GETTING PAID

*Legal Auditing and
Your Bottom Line*

D.L. SCHRADER

Getting Paid: Legal Auditing and Your Bottom Line

D.L. Schrader

Copyright © 2019 D.L. Schrader

All rights reserved. This book may not be reproduced in any form, in whole or in part (beyond the copying permitted by US Copyright Law, Section 107, "fair use" in teaching or research, Section 108, certain library copying, or in published media by reviewers in limited excerpts), without written permission from the author.

Disclaimer

This book is for educational purposes only. The views expressed are those of the author alone. The reader is responsible for his or her own actions. Adherence to all applicable laws and regulations, including international, federal, state, and local governing professional licensing, business practices, advertising, and all other aspects of doing business in the United States, Canada, or any other jurisdiction is the sole responsibility of the purchaser or reader. The author assumes no responsibility or liability whatsoever on the behalf of the purchaser or reader of these materials. Names, characters, places, and incidents are used fictitiously. Any resemblance to actual persons, living or dead, businesses, companies, events, or locales is entirely coincidental.

ISBN: 9781703284492

Imprint: Independently published

Book Layout & eBook Conversion by manuscript2ebook.com

Dedication

To my wife Elizabeth, my greatest champion and life partner. To Claire and John, the most wonderful children parents could ever have. And to my mother, whose unconditional love was more than any one person deserves. All have made me richer than any man could have ever hoped for.

Table of Contents

Dedication iii

Author's Note 1

Introduction 3

Chapter 1. **BLOCK BILLING**
 The Big Stumbling Block 5

Chapter 2. **VAGUE BILLING**
 Ohhh, Sweet Mystery of Life 23

Chapter 3. **THE "DIRTY THIRTY" OF LEGAL BILLING**
 *30 Words and Phrases
 To Use at Your Own Peril* 37

Chapter 4. **ADMINISTRATIVE AND CLERICAL WORK**
 *Do Not Pass Go. Do Not Collect
 (insert your hourly fee here)* 63

Chapter 5. **FORMULAS FOR DISASTER**
 Billing on Autopilot 75

Chapter 6. **LAW FIRM STAFFING AND
OFFICE COMMUNICATIONS**
The Gang is All Here *119*

Chapter 7. **BILLING JUDGMENT,
BILLING GUIDELINES AND APPEALS**
Understand, Plan, Prevail and Prosper *145*

About the Author 191

Author's Note

Over the last 20 years as a practicing attorney, then moving into the auditing field, I've had the good fortune to work with many great law firms, exceptional staff and truly dedicated attorneys.

Along the way, these folks have influenced and enhanced my career and I would like to thank them.

I've found that when working with law firms, administrative and billing staffs are hard-working diligent people who possess invaluable practical insight into the billing process, and I've become friends with many of them. If you want to know what is going on with a law firm's bills, talk to the staff. Once an auditor is a known quantity and they realize your goal is to partner with them and not "hide the ball" as it were, they will go out of their way to help you.

In my personal life, I've had the good fortune to have found a life partner, my wife, Elizabeth, a career legal secretary, who has operated as a sounding board and fount of information. Her insights into the billing methods and practices of some of the biggest law firms in the country have been instrumental throughout my auditing career and in the writing of this book.

Author's Note

Finally, a good book needs a great editor. I am blessed to have an editor equipped with the patience and persistence to make this work a functional guide while not damaging the writer's ego in the process. My thanks to Rebecca Schwartz, a master wordsmith, without whom I could not have completed this book.

Introduction

If you're reading this, you're likely a lawyer, paralegal or otherwise involved in the billing process at your firm. Whichever role, your mission is a simple one: You want to get paid every dime of what you bill.

However, your experience may likely be the opposite—you rarely get paid in full for your hard work. Why? Because either your client has hired their own legal auditor or they have engaged the services of a third-party legal auditing firm who has adjusted your time entries for any number of perceived infractions or violations of your client's billing guidelines and/or some other generally accepted billing principles.

My primary goal in writing this book, as an attorney and legal auditor with nearly 20 years of experience — both in-house and as a third-party legal auditor — is to give you the benefit of my knowledge — explain what you must do and not do in order to get paid for your efforts. While I can't tell you exactly what to say (you did the work so you only you know), I can and do tell you how to frame your description of the work in the best possible light in order to help you avoid getting your time cut and to get you paid in full. I do this by telling you what legal auditors

INTRODUCTION

are looking for and how you can use that to your benefit. By letting you get inside my head, you will gain an understanding of what the auditor, as your client's gatekeeper of legal fees, is focusing on as well as what you needn't be concerned with.

To be sure, this book is not intended to be a legal treatise on law firm billing, chock full of mind-numbing citations. Quite the contrary. My purpose is to provide you with a desk reference which you can quickly access for actionable advice on specific legal billing issues. And while I'll cite in a handful of cases for emphasis in some of the specific areas I cover, those authorities are used sparingly. My approach is to be as conversational and as candid as possible; the type of advice I provide attorney friends of mine when they are faced with rigorous billing guidelines and unforgiving auditors—to even the playing field.

Inside this book you will find examples of nearly every type of problematic billing issue that I've seen, culled from my review of more than a billion dollars in legal fees. This is shown by way of a Do this/Don't do that format, coupled with the rationale for each and how you can avoid the myriad of pitfalls lying in wait for the unwary.

My goal is to provide a concise and relevant guidebook that anyone from an experienced partner to a paralegal or new associate will reach for when grappling with the issue of how to meet each of their clients' billing expectations.

You work hard for your money. I want you to keep every dime of it that you properly have coming to you. What follows are my very best ideas and advice on how you can do just that.

Chapter 1

BLOCK BILLING

The Big Stumbling Block

Without a doubt, there is no more universally frowned upon legal billing issue than block billing. If block billing is a new term for you, this is what you need to know:

Block billing occurs when you've billed *more than one task* in a *single time entry* and then assigned a single amount of time for all of the tasks performed.

Even the most bare-bones client billing guidelines prohibit this practice. Why? Because your client (or whoever is responsible for paying your fees) cannot accurately determine the amount of time you spent on each of the tasks in the blocked entry. Consequently, it's virtually impossible for anyone to assess whether the time spent on any given task is overstated or inflated in any way. That's because the only person capable of actually quantifying the tasks in question — the attorney — has failed to provide the necessary detail.

BLOCK BILLING

Recognizing the uncertainty that block billing creates when attempting to evaluate the reasonableness of fees, many courts determined that the use of block billing may warrant a percentage reduction in — and in some cases a complete denial of — the fees sought. See, e.g., *Welch v. Metropolitan Life Ins. Co.*, 480 F.3d 942 (9th Cir. 2007); *In re Leonard Jed Company*, 103 B.R. 706, 713 (Bankr. D. Md. 1989); *Jane L. v. Norman H. Bangerter*, 61 F.3d 1505, 1510 (10th Cir. 1995). (Court reduced block billing fees by 35% stating, "Plaintiff's rather sloppy and imprecise time records failed to document adequately how plaintiff's attorneys utilized large blocks of time.")

Here is a typical example of a block-billed entry that I see on any given day:

> Draft Point 1 of Defendant's Motion for Summary Judgment; performed research regarding same; office conference with partner A. Smith regarding same; drafted e-mail to A. Smith re: same; attended telephone conference with A. Smith and client regarding progress and strategy on MSJ; drafted letter to client summarizing agreed strategy; office conference with S. Jones regarding arrangements for client meeting in Chicago.   6.40 hours

Well, now you've gone and done it. You have billed no less than seven — count 'em, seven — tasks in this single 6.40 hour time entry. BOOM!!!! Yes, most client billing guidelines will afford you an opportunity to appeal. But getting that money back is no sure thing either. First off, I've worked with some clients who've reduced block billed entries by as much as 50% and specifically denied the firm's ability to appeal.

While that may appear to be a harsh result, consider the issue from their perspective. Using the above example, how will the firm now assign time precisely to any of the seven tasks billed in the single time entry? The fact is that doing so is a factual impossibility if the time was not contemporaneously recorded. All that is left then is estimating that time. Your client is under no obligation to accept after-the-fact guesswork when it comes to billing.

Let's say that you are fortunate enough to have this time accepted without penalty. Consider for a moment the time involved in order to revise your time entries and all of the other hassle it's going to take you to appeal a reduction or a complete disallowance of those 6.40 hours. All of that time will be on your own dime and will *never* be compensated. Think about *that* for a moment.

It's absolutely critical then, that you take the time to jot down how much time was spent on *each* task. Otherwise, not only will you not be paid for your own time in having to draft an appeal response, but other firm personnel, including billing clerks, accounting staff or whoever in your firm deals with these issues in order to submit your appeal to the client will be diverted from more productive tasks. The cascade of wasted and unproductive time is solely traceable back to *you*.

Add to *your* uncompensated time that of other lawyers; perhaps even the partner you work for. If you think he or she won't mind, you'd be wrong, and I can't say that I'd blame them. To be fair, law schools don't even address billing, and law firms in my opinion only do a mediocre job at best. However, in the end, the responsibility (fair or not) falls squarely on your shoulders and no one else's.

All that said, rest assured that you are far from alone here. No one likes the administrative part of the practice of law and timekeeping is usually at the very top of that list. That's absolutely the way I felt about it too and I can commiserate with you 100% on this. But this isn't about me. This is about you getting paid and *paid in full* the first time — so let's get this right!

The truth of the matter is that most lawyers (and paralegals) live in a world of highly scrutinized billing — arguably the harshest time-clock gig on the planet. No minimum wage burger-flipper or factory line worker is so punished by time management as the legal profession. Unless today is your first day at the firm, you know that's the case. However, there's really nothing complicated here at all. It's one part mindset and one part common sense.

Let's take a moment and look at the narratives billed in the block billing example above and proceed on the basis that each is a separate and distinct task which should have been billed as such:

(1) "Draft Point I for Defendant's Motion for Summary Judgment."

Nothing problematic here except that I recommend that you should state what Point I is. While I cannot find fault with the description, in the case of possible duplicative work, the attorney with the clearest description generally goes unquestioned. You always want to be that person.

(2) "Performed initial research regarding same"

This is vague. Most clients require that the specific topic of the research be stated. Consider though if you had taken my advice regarding Point I above and stated what that Point was. An auditor *may* have then been able to reasonably infer what the research pertained to. But if he/she doesn't know what Point I was about then you won't get the benefit of that doubt. That said, never — and I mean never — count on the auditor to fill in the information for you. They do it. I do it. But it remains your responsibility regardless.

(3) "Office conference with partner A. Smith re: same."

Again, it's vague, as it fails to address the specific content of the conversation. Generally, clients don't want to pay for office conferences that relate to assigning tasks, for instance. Here, there's no way to tell. The mechanical phrase "re: same" is once again no help either. Same = Point I, and that's all anyone knows.

(4) "Drafted e-mail to A. Smith re: same"

Suggests exactly that — a memo from the associate to the partner addressing the "research". The seemingly endless parade of "re: same" is just as unsatisfying here. Has the associate even started the research? Is he stuck? Has he finished? Your guess is as good as mine.

(5) "Attended telephone conference with client and A. Smith regarding progress and strategy on MSJ."

Perfectly acceptable description.

[**Bonus Tip**: Some clients will disallow additional conferees who passively attend meetings or conferences. If you were at all involved in the discussion *leave no doubt* as to that fact by using the word "participate" instead of the word "attend."]

(6) "Drafted letter to client summarizing agreed strategy."

No issues here.

(7) "Office conference with paralegal S. Jones regarding arrangements for client meeting in Chicago."

Looks like an administrative communication to me. Sure, someone needs to schedule your flight and hotel room, but in most instances your client isn't going to pay for the time required to do that or for you to delegate the task (more on that later).

The point is that block billing won't shield you from other billing issues which are present. In fact, block billing creates doubt in the mind of your client or auditor, leaving you open to perhaps deeper scrutiny and removing any benefit of the doubt. If that weren't bad enough, I've personally witnessed the practice act as a negative catalyst which weakened the firm's relationship with the client. Losing money is one thing, losing a consistent paying client is another thing altogether.

You have to ask yourself, do I *really* need this headache? Of course you don't! Do this right the first time, no matter what a pain in the ass it seems, and avoid all of this potential grief.

The solution is simple: Do one task. Bill for that task. Rinse and repeat.

Stick with that and you cannot go wrong. Your life will be much easier, and you won't have to worry about any unpleasant surprises.

The Plural Trap

Never use these words in the plural form: Meeting, conference, correspondence, e-mail, discussion, call. The reason should be clear enough. While those words are fine, *meetings, conferences, correspondences, e-mails, discussions and telephone calls* immediately converts your time entry into a block billing issue.

My advice: Banish the plural usage of those words immediately!

I had a discussion not long ago with a billing clerk from a major firm. The partner she worked for didn't understand the above block billing issue and she was looking for an explanation from me.

I asked for an example from their latest invoice. She replied by directing me to the following time entry: "Discussions with opposing counsel regarding motion to compel."

She carried on for a minute about this not making sense and then I asked her, "What was the first word of that sentence?"

"Discussions," she replied.

"There's your answer," I told her. "Had that word been 'discussion' there would be no problem."

BLOCK BILLING

"Now wait a minute," she said, "Those discussions were about the same subject with the same person."

"Uh-huh," I replied.

"Seriously, I don't get it," she said, "What is your objection to that?"

"Okay," I replied, "Can you tell me how many 'discussions' the partner had with opposing counsel in the 1.40 hours he billed? Did he record somewhere how much time each discussion took?"

She had no idea and also opined that he most likely guesstimated the total throughout the day.

Setting aside the ethical propriety of guesstimating time, I explained that *the key point is that each and every discussion is a distinct and separate task which must be separately recorded*. The fact that the subject matter and other conferee are the same is irrelevant.

Do one task. Bill for one task. Follow that rule and block billing will never be an issue. The only exception I can conceive of is when a timekeeper completes multiple tasks in a tenth of an hour (0.10) or less. Given that tenth of an hour billing is the standard method of recording time, the issue becomes moot, but only in that scenario. However, in most instances when these plural words are used the time will be more than that, sometimes much more.

We wrapped up the call by discussing practical methods of recording and distinguishing the additional discussions. She made a good point by explaining that other attorneys have billed as I have advised here and their entries were adjusted as being duplicates.

I acknowledged that this can be a problem when both the subject matter and the amount of time billed are *identical*. This is certainly no fault of the attorneys but can and does result in erroneous adjustments to invoices for double-billing.

What to do? Probably the best method is to do so sequentially:

Second conference with opposing counsel, *Third* conference, *Fourth* conference, etc.

I say this fully realizing that you may have a dozen discussions in the same day, especially if you are negotiating a settlement, for instance. So if you're up to your "Twelfth conference with opposing counsel regarding settlement" you may be sick of this song and dance. However, at least you can cut and paste the same description and change only the first word while knowing that you are safe from any adjustments for block billing and/or double-billing.

Adjunct Tasks: Tag-Alongs

So what's this all about?

Be *very* careful with the word "and." It is generally not your friend. "And" for good reason. It is an insidious conjunction that can easily lull you into a block-billing trap if you are not careful; a gateway of sorts which leads to *including other closely related tasks in your single time entry.*

Example 1:

> Prepare *and* file Answer to Plaintiff's Complaint. 2.20 hours

It kills me every time I see this. And it's a safe bet that the lion's share of the time billed was for preparing the Answer.

However, you *tagged along* "and file" probably without much thought. I get it. This was the final step and it seemed only natural that you included the filing because it was such a closely related task. This now leaves you with a block billed time entry which also includes a non-billable administrative task (very few if any of your clients will allow payment for filing anything).

As a result, the auditor will likely have two choices: 1) Proportionalize each task and therefore 1.10 hours of that time isn't going in your pocket (at least not today), or 2) cut your entire 2.20 hour entry. Either way, you're not going to be happy and of course we want to avoid that.

The mindset you should strive to adopt, then, is compartmentalizing your work. To that end, think of legal billing as an assembly line of sorts. You've drafted the Answer, which is one widget and you've filed the Answer, which is yet another widget. When in doubt, break things up and assign time to each activity.

Example 2:

> Draft month-end report *and* distribute to the team for review and comment.   2.60 hours

Here, the auditor doesn't know if you e-mailed the report to the team or printed it out and went office-to-office with a pushcart and handed it to them. However, it doesn't really matter. What does matter is that you had a perfectly good entry for drafting the month-end report and the effort was derailed by including the distribution task, leaving your time technically block billed. Either the whole entry or a proportional amount could be deducted...even if it only took you 15 seconds to forward it to your distribution list. That's a heck of a steep price to pay.

Who would think that this three-letter conjunction could cause so many problems? Yet it does.

Example 3:

> Reviewed associate's research memorandum on defamation *and* plaintiff's discovery responses in order to draft L. Smith deposition outline.   3.40 hours

Example 3 is a curve-ball and is perfectly fine because it explains that you looked at more than one discrete document in order to draft the deposition outline, which was one separate and discreet task. A different scenario entirely. **You did *one* thing and properly billed for that one thing.**

Example 4:

> Researched defamation cases *and* drafted comprehensive research memorandum regarding same.   4.70 hours

Research and drafting a summary of findings are common tasks which are so closely related that it's no wonder they are often included together. Yet, Example 4 is nevertheless block billed. Research is a discrete task which should appear as a separate entry. The same is true with regard to drafting the summary memorandum. Additionally, most client billing guidelines

BLOCK BILLING

have limits on the number of hours which may be billed for research without approval. However, lumping both tasks together prevents the auditor from discerning the amount of time the research took from the added task of preparing the summary memorandum. Research is *always* a standalone task.

Example 5:

> Researched defamation cases *and* confer with partner V. Jennings re: same.   2.90 hours

Once again, these tasks *are* and *feel* so interrelated that it's natural for you to want to include them together. Nevertheless, it's still block billed. For many attorneys, some tasks seem so wedded to one another that they have simply fallen into a bad, yet completely understandable, rut.

The following four-word example is unquestionably the most common narrative that I read on an almost daily basis showing the issue.

Example 6:

> Prepare for *and* attend (hearing/deposition/client conference/trial, etc.)   7.20 hours

I get it. It's like peanut butter and jelly. Laverne and Shirley. Batman and Robin. Holy moly, Batman. I just got my bill cut! (Sorry, I couldn't resist!) But, in all seriousness, if you are in this habit you need to change it ASAP. No matter how related these tasks are they nonetheless stand on their own. **My recommendation:** Banish the use of this phrase forever!

Another common pitfall is joining travel time with event attendance as shown in the example below.

Example 7:

Travel to Washington, DC *and* attend expert interview of L. Stevens *and* return travel to New York.

Sure, it was a 16-hour day and it seemed natural to lump it all into the same bucket. However, some clients won't pay for your travel time or will only do so if you actually worked on the flight. Others may only pay you half rate. Regardless, while they are all related activities, the entry is nevertheless block billed. And since the auditor cannot know the precise amount of the travel time, the whole entry could be tossed out. It is really too burdensome to take a minute or so to break apart three things in a 16-hour day? You know the answer.

The key takeaway here is "and" is a word that can lull you into a block billing trap by causing you to "tag along" other related work into a single task; if you get careless using it, it will eventually burn you.

To avoid that result you **must** ask yourself this question: Does what comes after the word "and" refer to a separate task, or does it simply further describe the single task conducted? Asking that question could save you some serious dough and grief, or both.

The use of common punctuation also can lead to the same unpleasant results. Commas, colons, dashes, slashes, ellipses, etc., are all also potential pitfalls for the unwary.

All of the examples below are block billed:

Researched defamation cases, confer with partner V. Jennings re: same.

Draft Motion to Compel; e-mail to opposing counsel re: same.

Attend deposition of S. Lewis — confer with partner V. Jennings re: same.

Prepare for expert witness interview of B. Simms…conduct interview of expert B. Simms.

Frankly, you should *pause whenever you find yourself inserting ANY punctuation into your time entry*. It's generally a substitute for "and" anyway. Far more often than not, you'll discover that you're using punctuation to separate another task.

And God forbid you have multiple sentences. If your time entry looks like a paragraph you are most likely doing something wrong. Your goal should not be to reduce the number of time entries you have. Doing so may correspondingly reduce the number of dollars in your pocket.

Do it right. The first time. Get paid and get paid in full. *That* is what this is all about.

Embedded Time

Chances are that you would assume the following to be acceptable. And why not? You have assigned time to each task. Let's modify our original example:

Continued to draft Point 1 of Defendant's Motion for Summary Judgment (2.40); performed initial research regarding same (1.50); office conference with partner A. Smith regarding same (0.30); drafted memo to A. Smith re: same (0.60); attended telephone conference with A. Thomas and client regarding progress and strategy on MSJ (0.70); drafted letter to client summarizing agreed strategy (0.70); office conference with paralegal S. Jones regarding arrangements for client meeting in Chicago (0.20)   6.40 hours

Nothing objectionable with that, right? Wrong. It's like you ran the ball out of your own end-zone 95 yards but sat down 5 yards away from the goal-line.

You did all the heavy lifting by quantifying each distinct task but failed by not having each appear as a separate line item. It may seem like nit-picking; however, as noted above, your client's billing guidelines may not compensate you for giving a research assignment to an associate, or for discussing travel arrangements with your paralegal.

Let's assume that is the case and the client or their auditor wants to disallow those two tasks out of the 6.40 hours. The process now becomes more complicated because each will have to be addressed in your single time entry and the calculations will not add up to what was billed. "So what?" you say, "That's their problem." Not so fast. It now also becomes a problem for your firm's billing personnel because the numbers won't add up. Additionally, it may not be readily apparent to them which of the seven tasks are being objected to. So, in the end, it will more than likely *become* your problem.

Block Billing

The bottom line: Most clients will not accept this method of billing. Avoid it.

Is Block Billing ever acceptable?

The answer is maybe and yes.

Let me explain...

In the Maybe category, the reality is that if you bill low enough time (and there are no other billing issues present), many auditors are going to let it go.

Examples:

Telephone conference with client regarding trial setting and drafted letter to client regarding same. 0.20 hours

Drafted letter to Plaintiff's attorney regarding settlement and telephone call to client regarding same. 0.20 hours

In general, if I see a 1 to 1 ratio of tasks to tenths of an hour (e.g., two tasks in one entry billed at 0.20 hours), I'm going to let that go (please don't tell anyone!). But, go much beyond that and you're running the risk that you're going to get dinged for it, if nothing else because it's technically block billed.

While auditors don't set out to deliberately cause you grief, we're accountable and have to stand behind what we do as well as what we don't do. While I can justify overlooking these minor variations there are some strict constructionists in our little world. You've probably met at least one along the line. Hopefully, I don't usually fit that description, but I'm sure some days I deserve it.

Want to be sure and skip the roll of the dice? Then get it right to begin with by sticking with the fool-proof "Do one task, bill for one task" method.

On the Yes side of the equation, here is an **example of a block-billed entry that will always pass muster:**

Additional e-mails from and to client regarding settlement (*block-billed to reduce costs; individual entries would create a higher billable total*). 0.10 hours

Yes, sir. You are *really* looking out for your client's bottom line here. You're a star. And a rare one at that. The fact is, you *could* bill more but you chose not to. After all, *their* rules are mandating that each and every task appears as a separate line item entry, right?

Maybe you are already doing this. You bill a tenth of an hour to read your client's e-mail message and send a reply. Good for you. *My point is that you should be reminding your client that you're one of the good guys by doing these things.* Let them know you are focused on *their* bottom line, not yours. Do that by tooting your own horn in the way you craft your time entries. If it all happens behind the scenes no one is going to know, and (trust me) you want them to know!

These seemingly small things add up to create the perception that your ethics in billing match your ethics in lawyering. And *perception is everything.*

Key Tactics to Avoid Block Billing Adjustments

- Do one task — bill for one task.
- Avoid plural words (e.g., meetings, conferences, calls, emails, etc.).
- Pause every time you use the conjunction "and," then ask yourself "Is what comes next a separate task?"
- Every time you use punctuation such as a comma or colon, ask yourself, "Is what comes next a separate task?"
- Even if you assign time to each task, never do so in a single time entry— each must appear as a separate line item.
- If you perform multiple tasks in one-tenth of an hour (0.10) include language to the effect that you are doing so in order to avoid inflation of the time actually spent.

Chapter 2

VAGUE BILLING

Ohhh, Sweet Mystery of Life

In my world (the auditor's), far and away the most pervasive billing issue concerns vaguely described time entries. I never cease to be astonished at this, especially considering that the legal world relies so heavily on the ability to precisely use the written word to advance arguments in your clients favor.

Yet, sure as the sun will rise in the East, I see attorneys (and paralegals) bill for vagaries such as "Worked on case" or "Attention to matter," to name a few. If you think about it for a moment, you'd have to admit that neither of these phrases would inform anyone as to what work was performed.

Let's say that you take your car to the repair shop. You pick it up later in the day and you're handed a bill for $500. Not surprisingly you ask, "So, what was this for?" The shop looks at your bill and says, "See right there, sir? Our mechanic billed 3 hours at $100 per hour to 'Work on car' and another 2 hours at $100 per hour for 'Attention to car' — Is there a problem?" And, unless you have the IQ of a radish, you rightfully say, "You're darn right there is — I don't have the foggiest idea of exactly what I'm paying for and I'm not going to pay unless you provide me specific details of what the mechanic did."

Yet, the same attorney that would (legitimately) protest a bill like that from their mechanic would nonetheless blithely bill their client with a wholly uninformative description like "worked on case" or "attention to matter." And if that time was cut from their bill they might be indignant about it. "That was honest work and I expect to be paid for it!"

Maybe so, counselor, but if you wouldn't pay your mechanic's bill without a better description, what makes you think your client should pay yours if you have done no better? Because you're a lawyer and he's a mechanic? Well, of course not.

I've said it before but I can't stress this enough:

Your description is how you get paid!

Don't take my word for it though. As the court *In re Kroh Brothers Development Co.*, 105 B.R. 515, 525 (W.D. Mo. 1989), stated:

> The Court should not be required to indulge in guesswork, nor undertake extensive labor to justify a fee for an attorney who has not done so himself. We do not find it an unbearable burden to require an attorney seeking compensation to enlighten the Court as to the nature of his toil and the relation it bears to the matters at hand. **Absent such a statement, compensation may not be allowed.** [emphasis added]

Think about that for a moment: *"compensation may not be allowed."*

And why is that? Because the attorney's time entries lacked sufficient information to determine whether the fees for services rendered should be compensable.

There is only person who can justify the fee billed. That person is you.

Make no mistake; billing your time properly *is* part of the practice of law. Often overlooked or simply minimized, it's the last (essential) step in the process culminating in dollars in your bank account for all of your hard work.

Failure to do so properly can result in receiving less of those dollars or a delay in receiving them. Neither is good and what we're trying to avoid here.

With that in mind we turn back to the *unbearable burden* the Court referred to above, which means no more than asking you to write one detailed sentence. That's all. No more is necessary and no more is required.

So you ask, "Just what do you mean by a **vague** time entry and what can I do to avoid my own entries from being characterized as such?"

Vague work comes in two forms: Vague task descriptions and vague communications. I'll address the latter first because the remedy is quite simple.

Vague Communications

Every communication of any kind — telephone conference, e-mail, letter or meeting *must* do at least these 2 things:

1) **Identify the other party or parties involved (and ideally their role(s) in the matter).**
2) **Identify the subject matter and/or purpose of the communication.**

Yet, for some reason still unknown to me, the amount of time entries I review which are missing one or both requirements is, quite frankly, shocking.

Let's take a look at our basic vague communication example: "Conference with Smith."

While I know who you are because your name is at the end of the line following your time entry, that's about it. I don't know who Smith is. Is she a claims representative? An associate at your firm working on the matter? Opposing counsel? The owner of the deli from whom you're ordering a tuna sandwich on whole wheat?

Now, in all likelihood the auditor or whoever is reviewing the bill is going to recognize some names — at least the names from their own organization. And perhaps there will be a Smith somewhere within that group, but that's not the point.

The point is that you cannot and should not make any assumptions regarding what or who your reader or the auditor knows. Given that *only you know* who you are communicating with it is incumbent upon you to identify the other party or parties involved.

The following examples are **unacceptable** because the conferee(s) have not been identified:

- Meeting regarding insufficient discovery responses.
- Conference regarding trial preparation.
- E-mail regarding possible motion for sanctions.
- Telephone call regarding testimony.

Likewise, failure to include the subject matter as in the examples below yields the same result.

- Meeting with opposing counsel Jackson.
- Conference with associate Williams.
- E-mail with client Morris.
- Telephone call with expert witness Stevens.

Failure to include both the subject matter as well as the identity of the other party or parties being communicated with is a surefire way to get your bill slashed.

- Meeting
- Conference
- E-mail
- Telephone call

I refer to this kind of biller as The Minimalist. The Minimalist is a favorite target for the auditor. It's almost like shooting ducks in a barrel. Sure, you saved a few keystrokes, but at what cost? Remember, one descriptive sentence is all you need. No one is asking for more than what you see below.

- Meeting with opposing counsel Jackson regarding discovery responses.
- Conference with associate Williams regarding trial preparation.
- E-mail with client Morris regarding possible motion for sanctions.
- Telephone call with expert witness Stevens regarding testimony.

The communications formula is simple: [Communicate] with _____ regarding _____.

To be 100% clear, you do **not** want to use the word *communicate*. I use the word only to reference all of the different forms of communication, ranging from e-mails to telephone calls to internal and external meetings. Always be specific about what form of communication was utilized.

Aside from vague communications, the next major pitfall to avoid is *vague task descriptions*.

Vague Task Descriptions

You know what task you performed but that information isn't translating into the words that make up your time entry. And, as mentioned, it could cost you dearly, too. One might think that fact alone would cause this problem to all but disappear. Yet it hasn't and shows no sign of abating anytime soon.

One major contributor to the problem is the mistaken reliance upon certain verbs and a (mistaken) assumption that the verb itself is enough to tell the story of the work performed. In fact, there are verbs that in my opinion you should avoid ever using for that reason alone. Most of those I will discuss in detail in the next chapter, but one is so problematic I feel compelled to address it here.

That verb (and various forms of it which follow) is far too useful to eliminate from your billing vocabulary. However, it's so often at the center of time entries identified as vague that I would be remiss if I didn't give it special attention here.

Prepare/Preparation

Now, let's be candid about this. As an attorney, I (probably) know what you did to prepare for trial or for a hearing or deposition. But that doesn't make any difference. Remember, the auditor isn't supposed to assume anything, though some of that is nonetheless inevitable.

Preparing largely comes in two forms — review or drafting and possibly both. When it comes to any kind of preparation, the auditor wants to know specifically *what* you reviewed or drafted in order to prepare for whatever event you attended.

Do this:

Example 1:

Prepare for trial *by* reviewing all deposition transcripts, motions and pleadings.

VAGUE BILLING

Example 2:

Prepare for inspection *by* reviewing factual background and expert Jennings' report.

Example 3:

Prepare for plaintiff Crawford's deposition *by* drafting outline of questioning.

Here's your rule:

Any sentence with the word "prepare" should also include the word "by."

The narrative form is always: "Prepared for _____ by reviewing/drafting _____."

Do not do this:

Example 4:

Prepare for trial.

This example fails because there is no preposition — "*by*" — which describes the specifics of what the attorney did to *prepare* for trial.

Or this:

Example 5:

Prepare for trial by reviewing file materials.

Nice try. But your reference to reviewing "file materials" left you in no better position than if you had said, "Prepare for trial." Which file materials did you review? There's no way to know based on the description. The point is that you can't fill in the blank with just anything and expect that to be acceptable. Please... SHARE THE DETAILS. You don't have to list every document reviewed, either. No one expects that. Just give the auditor something to go on, like the example below:

Do this:

Example 6:

> Prepare for trial by reviewing all pleadings, motions, and relevant communications.

Done! Again, one concise statement and you're good to go.

Suffice to say that the Highway of Vagueness is littered with many words and phrases which, in my opinion, you should severely limit or eliminate altogether from your legal billing vocabulary. Avoiding those will make your life much easier. Not doing so will most assuredly cause you grief and frustration. I don't want that for you. You can find many of those in the next chapter of this book.

But first, let's examine some other scenarios which either dilute or unnecessarily complicate your time entries. **Clear and concise** — that's the goal.

Vague Tag Lines

Here we're talking about entries in which the primary task is perfectly fine but the *added task* description is vague.

Example 1:

> Review proposed settlement agreement and prepare for further handling.

What does "prepare for further handling" mean? I have no idea and no one else would either.

Example 2:

> Researched Daubert standard and performed related tasks.

Which related tasks? I can make a few educated guesses but guesswork is not your friend.

Of course, both examples are also block billed. However, even if you escaped having the entries adjusted for block billing they may yet fail for vagueness.

In sum, every word counts.

Unnecessary Tag Lines

These phrases do not add value to the service you provide. They are nothing but unnecessary justifications for your time. Your objective is to leave no doubt that you have provided a fully compensable service. Please — just the facts and no more.

Examples:

> Draft expert Wells' witness outline for upcoming deposition *and do so in accordance with our defense efforts.*

> Review expert Wells' report for upcoming deposition *in furtherance of the defense of this matter.*

Take expert Wells' deposition *for purposes of the continued defense of this matter*.

Don't waste your time stating the obvious — it's assumed that EVERYTHING you do should be furthering the defense of the case.

Mr. Vague: The Master of Acronyms

I get it. Shorthand can be a wonderful thing. To make it through 19 years of schooling, or however many you went through, it was a necessary skill for survival. And, unless you were sharing your notes with someone else, you were the only person who actually needed to understand them.

Enter the world of the practice of law. You may be fortunate enough to have someone else enter your time, leaving them to read your scribble or listen to your dictation. More likely, you are doing it yourself. Regardless of the method employed, it's ultimately your responsibility to be clear.

Unfortunately, there are those among the bar that insist on passing along their shorthand descriptions in their billing narratives.

Example:

RV RFP/ROGS RCVD FRM P ATTY.

WTF? Yeah, you know what that means. Listen, I hate to keep pounding this drum but the auditor is under no obligation whatsoever to decipher your meaning, even if it wouldn't take much effort on their part. Courts and client billing guidelines universally require your description to be readable by the average Joe. Expect Joe to have the same reaction I stated above. Yes, you may be able to fix the issue after-the-fact by submitting an appeal to your client. But who really wants to do that? We're talking about you having to re-write your time entries and wait another month or more to be compensated.

[**Bonus Tip**: For God's sake, please do NOT write your time entries in all CAPS. I regularly review invoices from some firms whose entire bills are in CAPS. It's completely obnoxious and frankly almost painful to have to read. Amazing that you wouldn't do that on social media but you'd force someone else to read through pages of all-capitalized text. It suggests to the reader/auditor that you really don't care. This, of course, is not the message you want to convey, especially to those in a position to approve or deny your bill. In instances of a close call you're not putting yourself in a position to receive the benefit of the doubt.]

Mr. Vague: The No Verb Guy

I know him fondly by such classic entries as:

- Motion for Protective Order
- Witness deposition
- Settlement

Okay, so at least we know the subject matter. But after that, all bets are off. Here, the lack of a verb in the description is a fatal flaw. You may believe that the task performed should be self-evident, but in isolation it is not.

Did you review or draft the Motion for Protective Order? Maybe you argued it? Did you take the expert witness deposition? Defend it? Schedule it? Prepare for it? Did you attend a Settlement Conference? Negotiate settlement by way of a conference call with plaintiff? The possibilities are almost endless.

There should never be any doubt as to *what* you're doing and *how* you're doing it — you can't do that without a verb. This one should be a slam-dunk.

Descriptive Overkill: The Serial Verb Guy

This is the alter-ego of the No Verb Guy. Technically, there is no actual problem with respect to the entry below because only one-tenth of an hour was billed. However, when more time is billed you could possibly find yourself with a block billing problem.

Example:

Read, review, revise, alter, amend, supplement, finalize and execute Notice of Deposition of Plaintiff Smith.

Details are one thing but *descriptive overkill is entirely unnecessary and only serves to dilute your narrative and may actually call it into question.* Here, the attorney used eight verbs to describe the task. Could he have used less verbiage and made it clearer? The answer is, of course he could have.

How about:

Review, revise and execute Notice of Deposition of Plaintiff.

Looks good...except:

[**Bonus Tip**: *Never* bill to execute a document. If you are reviewing or revising your work, leave it at that. However, if you are simply putting your signature on the document, do not bill for it. I mean, how many seconds did it take to do that? It makes an attorney look a bit petty by appearing to squeeze out a few more bucks just because he/she can. It's simply not worth it in my opinion.]

Key Tactics to Avoid Vague Billing Adjustments

- Your description is everything when it comes to getting paid.
- All entries for communications must include: 1) the identity of other party or parties being communicated with and 2) the subject matter and/or purpose of the communication.
- Any entry for "preparation" should include the word "by" explaining exactly what you did in order to "prepare."
- Avoid vague tag lines or descriptions (e.g., "and prepare for further handling").
- Avoid unnecessary tag lines or descriptions (e.g., "in furtherance of this matter").
- Do not use acronyms.
- Do not write in CAPS.
- Your entry must contain a verb.

Chapter 3

THE "DIRTY THIRTY" OF LEGAL BILLING

30 Words and Phrases To Use at Your Own Peril

These are words and phrases which lack the specificity your client requires in a descriptive time entry. While *you* know exactly what work you performed, your choice of words needs to communicate that information. Doubt and ambiguity are your enemies when it comes to successful billing. Clear, specific and transparent wording is your goal in each time entry

Consider banishing the use of many of these words and phrases altogether. They are a trap for the unwary and if you think about it, you will conclude that they are not good choices for the purpose. The purpose is to write precisely so that your work is not questioned.

Initially, these words and phrases may appear perfectly acceptable, but as we'll soon see, they almost always leave the auditor scratching their head and wondering "What exactly did she do here?" At that point, it's over. You've performed valuable and compensable work but by using the wrong choice of words, you've failed from a billing perspective.

Of course, it's not so much that these words are actually "dirty"; it's that they are used consciously or unconsciously as a form of shorthand. I believe that more often than not it's the latter. Since you did the work, you know exactly what you've done; therefore it seems only natural that your reader would as well.

More attention to detail and the addition of a few well-chosen words is extra effort that will absolutely pay off. However, neglect these details and you'll end up having far more work dealing with audit adjustments than if you had got it right the first time. You don't need the hassle and grief of having to argue that you should have been paid in full to begin with. It's my hope that what follows will help you do just that.

The good news is that many of these words and phrases could be rehabilitated simply by including the phrase "by [doing] _____." And that is where attorneys and paralegals are dropping the ball. Which is unfortunate, when a few more words could make a world of difference. Assuming you choose the right words. On the other hand, some of these words can't be rehabilitated. There's simply no advice I can give you to fix them. Regardless, it's vitally important in my opinion that I point them out so that you're aware of the potential pitfalls.

With all that in mind, let's get at it!

1. Attention to

Don't write this:

Attention to Motion for Summary Judgment.

When I see "Attention" or "Attention To," I visualize someone looking or staring at something. Perhaps she is looking over at her first draft of the motion sitting at the edge of her desk and she's thinking, "I really don't want to work on that right now!" But seriously, the point is that this is an uninformative phrase because it doesn't describe exactly what you're doing. The auditor knows the subject matter, but not the precise task you are engaged in concerning it. The conjunction "by" below makes all the difference.

Write this:

Attention to Motion for Summary Judgment by drafting Statement of Facts.

2. Follow Up

Don't write this:

Follow up regarding Motion to Dismiss.

Ask yourself, what does the phrase really tell you? The reader understands that the subject matter is the Motion to Dismiss but they don't know what work was undertaken in order to follow up. Once again, the conjunction "by" is your ally here.

Write this:

Follow up regarding Motion to Dismiss by adding substantive revisions to associate A. Lange's first draft of same.

3. Work On

Don't write this:

Work on Motion for Summary Judgment.

"Work on" is the third part of the trifecta of the most common generic phrases (along with "attention to" and "follow up") that attorneys trip up on. To be blunt, your "work" is assumed with regard to any task appearing in your time entries. What's missing is the specific description of that work. The auditor wants to know if you've drafted it, researched it, filed it or spoke to your client about it. And — you guessed it — adding "by [doing] _____" is the key.

Write this:

Work on Motion for Summary Judgment by conducting legal research on similar 8th Circuit Court cases.

4. Consider

Don't write this:

Consider response to Plaintiff's 2nd Amended Complaint.

Like the word "strategize" (#24 below), the word works better when you're in a conference setting (e.g., "Inter-office conference with case team to briefly consider response to Plaintiff's

2nd Amended Complaint."). However, when it's used to describe a solitary task, your client may assume you're reclining in your office chair with your feet on the desk, ruminating about the issue. (Just between you and me, if that was precisely what you were doing and it resulted in an "Aha!" moment, it could be the most valuable activity you could perform.) Adding a few details regarding the specifics of your "consideration" as in the example below will remove any connotation of vagueness.

Write this:

> Consider response to Plaintiff's 2nd Amended Complaint through review of initial Complaint and our response to same in preparation for drafting reply.

5. Determine

Don't write this:

> Determine best course of action with regard to settlement offer from plaintiff's attorney J. Morrison.

How did you determine the best course of action with regard to plaintiff's settlement offer? Chances are you were contemporaneously reviewing something or drafting ideas — ALWAYS include those details when using a word like this.

Write this:

> Determine best course of action with regard to settlement offer from plaintiff's attorney J. Morrison by reviewing her prior correspondence concerning settlement, as well as pertinent pleadings and discovery responses to date.

6. Manage
[Similar words to avoid: Supervise, Oversee]

Don't write this:

Manage case progress.

As vital as your management skills may be to any given matter, your clients invariably don't want you to **bill** them for tapping into that skillset. (Sorry, I don't make the rules here.) That said, if what you're doing is not pure management, then focus on the specifics of whatever that other thing is and leave the "manage" out of your time entry description altogether.

Write this:

[Managed case by] drafting memorandum to client regarding current case status; suggested actions to move case forward.

7. Address

Don't write this:

Address problems identified in our expert's (J. Baker) report.

Like so many of the words and phrases "addressed" in this chapter, it's inadequate without further elaboration. Unfortunately, far more often than not, that key information has been left out, leaving the auditor wondering exactly what task was performed. But by adding "by [doing] _____" to the above example you should be fine. Are you noticing a theme here? Good!

Write this:

> Address problems identified in our expert's report by reviewing plaintiff's expert report and drafting discussion points in preparation for roundtable with client (D. Lange) and trial team.

8. Issues

Don't write this:

> Discuss issues regarding deposition of defense witness (Williams) with associate Anderson.

An uninformative word if ever there was one. Standing on its own, it tells the auditor nothing regarding the specific deposition "issues" discussed with associate Anderson. It *could be* something as basic as a scheduling issue or it could be a substantive issue. That distinction often matters when it comes to in-firm communications. However, because the auditor cannot assume what the subject matter is, you need to flesh this out in order to avoid your time entry becoming the "issue" instead of the actual communication.

Write this:

> Discussion with associate Anderson regarding conflicting statements made by defense witness (Williams) and potential issues as a result of same for his upcoming deposition.

9. Forward
[Similar words to avoid: Circulate, Disseminate]

Don't write this:

> Forward discovery documents as requested to client (Hanson).

Let me re-phrase that. If the *only* thing you did was forward a document, then that is precisely what you should write. One of my prior clients actually wrote a provision in their billing guidelines which stated that they considered billing for forwarding documents to be "offensive." Kind of strong, but I suppose I get it. On the other hand, if you are forwarding documents of any kind *and* have a substantive comment to make (not "see attached") then make it clear that you are doing so. It completely changes the nature of your time entry.

Write this:

> Forward discovery documents as requested to client (Hanson) with my thoughts on responding to same.

10. Materials
[Similar words to avoid: Documents]

Don't write this:

> Prepared "materials" for deposition of plaintiff.

Here we have another "dirty" word that causes nothing but grief in most instances. "Materials" almost always refers to an unspecified document or documents of some kind and that's the problem. This is one of those words that you should banish from your lexicon, unless you're using it as an adjective (e.g., material witness).

Write this:

> Prepared and revised exhibits in preparation for upcoming deposition of plaintiff.

11. Action taken

Don't write this:

> Action taken regarding supplementing discovery responses.

The issue here is that the auditor doesn't know what action was taken. It would be a reasonable assumption that the "action taken" is what comes next in the description, which would be that the attorney drafted the discovery responses. Maybe she did and maybe she didn't. However, the auditor has no basis to come to that conclusion given what has been described here. You'd be better off avoiding this phrase altogether; instead, describe the specific action you took with regard to the discovery responses.

Write this:

> Drafted supplemental interrogatory answers.

12. Assist

Don't write this:

> Assist associate with Plaintiff's document production requests.

Permit me, if you will, to assist by advising that this "dirty" word is of no assistance to you. Yes, you can use it but, by itself, it's too generic. It's always best to cut right to the chase. Either remove the word or use it and include our new best friend "by [doing] _____."

Write this:

Assist associate with Plaintiff's document production requests by drafting responses to questions 1-20.

Even better:

Drafted responses to questions 1-20 of plaintiff's requests for production of documents.

13. Discovery

Don't write this:

Conference with plaintiff's attorney regarding discovery issues.

We all know what it is but it's used too often in the broadest sense. Let's pair it with the previously discussed "dirty" word — issues. That phrase leaves the auditor wanting more as it's doubly vague. It's like seeing your doctor and having her say, "I'm afraid you have a medical issue." "Uh, could you possibly narrow that down for me, doctor?" What specific aspect of discovery are you talking about and what is the specific issue? The money (or lack of it) is always in the details.

Write this:

> Conference with plaintiff's attorney regarding his failure to adequately respond to our interrogatory requests and whether motion to compel will be necessary.

14. Monitor

Don't write this:

> Monitor progress of drafting Motion for Summary Judgment.

For me, the word invariably evokes recollections of high school and college "monitors" who did nothing more that occupy a seat to make sure people were well behaved and/or not cheating on an exam. It's generally a *passive* term which requires no more than being awake. As you might have surmised by now, the standards for successful legal billing are much higher. Choose more *active* words where possible. What did you specifically do in order "monitor" progress on the Motion for Summary Judgment?

Write this:

> Meeting with Associate D. Fowler to review his progress on the Motion for Summary Judgment and provide substantive input regarding revising same.

15. Prepare/Preparation

This "dirty" word (also addressed in Chapter Two) may be responsible for more grief for lawyers and paralegals than any other word that I can name. Attorneys and paralegals fall prey to the mistaken assumption that the word conveys all that need be stated. They could not be more wrong. So let's fix this once and for all.

For paralegals, the usage generally involves doing something *to* another thing (as in the example below).

Don't write this:

> Prepare documents at the request of associate V. Smithson in advance of next week's scheduled trial.

Does the *preparation* primarily involve copying, retrieving, gathering or organizing documents? Or is something more substantive involved? As always, it's about applying **legal** knowledge. *If* you are using your legal knowledge as opposed to performing a rote ministerial task then by all means put the focus on *that*.

Write this:

> Prepared witness transcripts by highlighting relevant testimony in advance of associate V. Smithson's review.

For attorneys, the usage generally involves doing something *for* another thing/purpose (as in the example below).

Don't write this:

> Prepare for hearing on Plaintiff's Motion to Compel.

Many attorneys have fallen into the rut of assuming that the reader knows what the attorney is doing when they are preparing for such things as hearings, meetings, depositions, trial, arbitrations/mediations, etc. Truth be told, I could in most instances fill in the blanks and be right far more often than I'd be wrong. However, filling in the blanks is not the auditor's job, it's yours. A handful of extra words are all that is required. C'mon, you got this!

Write this:

> Prepare for hearing on Plaintiff's Motion to Compel by reviewing motion as well as all discovery correspondence to-date.

16. Scheduling

Don't write this:

> Telephone conference with plaintiff's attorney regarding scheduling depositions of remaining witnesses.

By now you've probably realized that the above narrative probably won't make it past the client's auditor without being labeled as a secretarial task. The description conjures up a conversation with two attorneys who have their calendars in front of them with no more involved than deciding on mutually acceptable dates. And if that is all that is involved, then I can't help you. However, I do have a tip and here it is: **Add a substantive component to your scheduling discussion whenever you possibly can.** That will force the auditor to give you credit for the time because it's a single conference which can't be sliced and diced. Works like a charm every time.

Write this:

Telephone conference with plaintiff's attorney regarding scheduling depositions of remaining witnesses as well as when we can expect to receive his client's answers to our 2nd Amended Interrogatories or whether a Motion to Compel will be necessary.

17. Efforts

Don't write this:

Efforts to reach compromise in discovery dispute.

No one is going to question that this task is substantive and important. However, the auditor is going to pose one question: "What specific efforts did you undertake in order to reach a compromise in this situation?" It's a safe bet that some sort of communication took place, but what was it? If you had a conference call with the plaintiff's attorney in order to reach a compromise regarding the discovery dispute, then say so to begin with. Otherwise, your *efforts* may all be for naught.

Write this:

Discovery conference call held with plaintiff attorney B. Adams wherein agreement was reached with regard to our document production requests.

18. Tend to

Don't write this:

Tend to completion of responses to requests for production.

I know you are practicing law, but this phrase makes it appear more like you're gardening. "Tend to" your zucchini and squash; stick with the specifics and avoid indefinite words and phrases such as this. Enough said.

Write this:

Drafted and edited our responses to Plaintiff's Requests for Production of Documents.

19. Solicit

Don't write this:

Solicit suggestions from trial team regarding strategy for cross-examination of forensics expert.

If you're asking for input then please say so and *always* use the most precise wording in describing the *method* of communication utilized (e.g., e-mail, letter, telephone, in-person meeting, etc.)

Write this:

Draft detailed e-mail to trial team asking for their input with regard to strategy for the cross examination of plaintiff's forensics expert.

20. Pursue

Don't write this:

Pursue settlement.

I tend to be a visual person. When I read this my mind conjures up images of a chase scene, wherein our hero (the attorney) is chasing after the bad guy who is wearing a shirt that says "settlement" on it. Now I'm not sure what actually happens when our hero finally catches "settlement" — I can't quite picture that, but I hope he goes easy on the guy. Maybe just object to his bad taste in attire. Seriously though, I can't imagine one good use for this word in a legal setting.

Write this:

Drafted detailed e-mail to plaintiff's attorney T. Jacobs regarding my thoughts on his recent settlement overtures.

21. Next Steps

Don't write this:

Consideration of next steps in the matter.

The literalist might assume you're out for a stroll on the sidewalk outside your office building while you're pondering your next legal move in the case. Okay, the phrase itself is fine; it's what you pair the phrase with that matters. The point is that you need to express *how* you considered those next steps. **Always** identify any document(s) you are utilizing with regard to any kind of analysis or evaluation you are engaging in.

Write this:

In consideration of next steps regarding possible motion to compel, reviewed plaintiff's responses to our second interrogatories.

22. Various

Don't write this:

Various telephone conferences with court clerk regarding postponement of preliminary hearing.

Especially when coupled with communication-based tasks, this plural word will invariably lead to adjustments for block billing reasons. It is also vague. How many telephone conferences was that? Who knows? The word is also uninformative in other contexts as well (e.g., "Review of *various* documents in preparation for interview of witness A. Washington.") Pardon me, but which documents were those? Remove this word from your billing lexicon now and you will thank me later.

Write this:

Telephone call from court clerk regarding postponement of preliminary hearing.   0.20 hours

Additional telephone call from court clerk confirming postponement of preliminary hearing.   0.20 hours

23. Communicate/Communication

Don't write this:

Communicate with trial team regarding order of witnesses.

I can hear it now, "What on earth could possibly be wrong with a description like that?" The issue is that the word "communicate" is imprecise. It's a catch-all word for different forms of communication, including e-mail, telephone calls and in-person meetings. While it may be a safe bet for you to assume that the auditor will rule out that you used two tin cans and a long string, a carrier pigeon, or perhaps smoke signals, you can't make any assumptions beyond that. The pitfalls may not be obvious but they are nevertheless real. Auditors will match up things like e-mails and in-firm conferences for anything from content to seeing how much time each timekeeper billed in order to find discrepancies and/or ambiguities. If you were in a meeting, then use that word to describe the specific form of communication utilized. Being precise in billing is your objective here.

Write this:

In-firm meeting with trial team regarding order of witnesses.

24. Strategize
[Similar words to avoid: Contemplate, Consider]

Don't write this:

Strategize regarding handling in light of new arbitrator assigned to case.

As a solitary task (not used in a conference situation) you can come off as appearing to be Rodin's *The Thinker*. Maybe you're looking at something? Maybe you're writing something down? I understand the thought process. However, you need to be able to describe that in a more tangible way, especially if a significant amount of time is billed. Look, I know you're doing something more than resting your head on your desk. However, to avoid any assessment as being vague or uninformative I'm suggesting that the best practice would be to follow the word up with what you do next.

Write this:

> Strategize regarding handling in light of new arbitrator assigned to case by reviewing associate's summary of the arbitrator's decisions in similar cases.

25. Re: same

Don't write this:

> Inter-office conference with associate J. Williams re: same.

On the one hand the phrase is perfectly fine, but *if and only if* it is 100% clear what the "re: same" is referring to. If the subject does not follow the preceding time entry or is not obviously related to it, then you could have a potential problem. You might have ten time entries on a particular day and if the "re: same" in the tenth entry refers to the subject matter of your third entry on that date, then that's not good. You don't want the auditor to go out of his/her way to connect-the-dots and have to glean what the discussion was about. Your shorthand should not make the auditor's job any harder than it is already. If you like certainty, then use the tried-and-true method of avoiding doubt by including the subject matter.

Write this:

> Inter-office conference with associate J. Williams regarding deposition of fact witness K. Lewis and inconsistencies in his testimony.

26. And

Don't write this:

Drafted Motion for Sanctions and conference call with client re: same.

If you skipped over Chapter 1 on Block Billing then you're probably asking yourself, "What is this guy smoking? This makes no sense." That is, until you really think about the example above. The three-letter conjunction "and" joins two *separate and distinct* tasks. With regard to block billing considerations, it is irrelevant that those tasks are related. What is relevant is that you drafted a motion, which was one task that took x number of minutes and/or hours to prepare, and either before or after that you had a conference call with your client about it.

This is not to say that you can't use "and" in any number of contexts:

Example:

Prepared for plaintiff's deposition by reviewing pleadings and discovery responses.

Example:

Drafted updated case summary for client by reviewing all correspondence to date **and** research memorandum regarding prospects for successful appeal of decision.

Note the difference. It is important.

Write this:

Drafted Motion for Sanctions.

Write this:

> Conference call with client regarding our Motion for Sanctions.

27. Instructions
[Similar words to avoid: Assignment]

Don't write this:

> Instructions to associate Anderson regarding tasks to be completed before deposition of plaintiff's forensic expert (C. Wallace).

While teachable moments can be extremely important, anything resembling teaching, on-the-job training or tote-that-barge-and-lift-that-bale communications are not only frowned upon, but specifically disallowed in many client billing guidelines. Yes, this ignores reality, especially with regard to newer associates. It also ignores how things get done. As an attorney once said to me, "How is the associate supposed to divine what I'd like her to do?" Darn good point, don't you think? Rules are rules though, and my recommendation is to avoid this word if you can. While you're at it, skip the word "task" as well and get straight to the description. Same information but framed differently. See the difference?

Write this:

> Discussion with [or "Memorandum to"] associate Anderson regarding specifics of research and investigation needed before deposition of plaintiff's forensic expert (C. Wallace).

28. Exchange

Don't write this:

> Exchange emails with partner (D. Wagner) regarding strategy in questioning plaintiff's expert.   0.40 hours
> [L. Rudolph]

The issue here is a simple yet galling one to most attorneys and I understand that frustration. However, the unmistakable fact is that, by definition, multiple communications took place in one time entry. This leaves you wide open to an adjustment for block billing, unless that "exchange" took only a tenth of an hour. Again, I agree that it can be obnoxious to have to write multiple entries for back-and-forth communications, especially when the same subject matter is involved. However, the fact is that the word is a potential landmine and I don't want to see you step on it.

Write this:

> Draft email to partner (D. Wagner) regarding strategy in questioning plaintiff's expert.   0.20 hours
> [L. Rudolph]

> Review response from partner (D. Wagner) regarding his thoughts on questioning plaintiff's expert.   0.10 hours
> [L. Rudolph]

> Draft follow-up email to partner (D. Wagner) regarding his thoughts on questioning plaintiff's expert.   0.10 hours
> [L. Rudolph]

29. Numerous

Don't write this:

> Reviewed numerous e-mails from plaintiff attorney regarding settlement.   0.70 hours

Don't write this:

> Reviewed numerous banking records received from client.   3.90 hours

How many is "numerous"? The Merriam-Webster dictionary says that it consists of "great numbers of units." In the first scenario above I would ask whether you really reviewed *that many* emails. In fairness, the warning here depends on whether you read them all at once (e.g., you were in court all day and read them all in one fell swoop at the end of the day); or, you read them *separately* but lumped them together for purposes of convenience. In that case the former is perfectly fine but the latter would be considered block billing.

Write this:

> [List each settlement email separately. I won't do so here for the sake of brevity, but the point is to list them separately or risk being subject to reductions for block billing.]

In the second scenario above you can use the word to describe the number of documents reviewed. However, the better practice, especially when you bill multiple hours for such a task, is to give an approximation of the number of documents reviewed. Even saying "reviewed one-inch thick stack of financial records" would be more effective.

Write this:

> Reviewed approximately 500 pages of banking records received from client.   3.90 hours

30. Confirm

Don't write this:

> Confirmed that deposition of plaintiff's fact witness Harris has been cancelled.

Use of this word (for billing purposes) comes down to context. If the confirmation is related to scheduling as in the above example it will likely be disallowed as administrative work. The same would also be true if you billed to confirm that *your* firm has completed a given task. On the other hand, confirming what the opposing party or a third party has done or not done may be another situation, with the caveat that you need to describe *how* you confirmed that.

Write this (different context):

> Telephone conference with plaintiff's attorney (Jones) to confirm that his settlement proposal will be forthcoming.

And if you want to bootstrap the scheduling confirmation example above into a *paid* entry then **write this:**

> Telephone conference with plaintiff's attorney (Jones) to confirm that his settlement proposal will be forthcoming and also confirmed that the deposition of their fact witness (Harris) has been cancelled.

Honorable Mentions

While we limited our consideration to 30 words out of the entire English language, many other words could have made that list, as they should be used cautiously or avoided altogether. In light of this, I have included below some other words and phrases which I routinely see as problematic, of which you should at least be aware.

"Dirty" Word or Phrase	Reason
Arrange	Administrative connotations.
Assemble	Almost always considered to be clerical work.
Attempt/Attempted	Generally not billable (e.g. "attempted phone call").
Bates-Stamp	Clerical work.
Calendar	Administrative work.
Coordinate	Administrative work.
Deal With	Uninformative.
File	Filing anything is generally not billable.
General File Review	Lacks specific focus and has a "make-work" connotation.
Google/Googled	Non-legal fact research. Can be billable but avoid the reference.
Plan/Planning	Administrative connotations. Requires clear and specific details.
Print	Clerical work.
Proofread	Clerical work (If you are also "revising" use that word instead).

THE "DIRTY THIRTY" OF LEGAL BILLING

Pull	Clerical work (e.g. "pull documents from client files").
Tie-Up	Vague (e.g. "Tie-up loose ends after trial").
Track Down	Clerical.
Train/Training	Administrative.
To-Do	Administrative (e.g. Draft "To–Do" list).
Upload/Download	Administrative/clerical non-legal work.
War Room	Clerical (e.g. "Prepare "War Room" for trial").

In sum, while no list can ever be exhaustive, being cognizant of these particular words and phrases and the negative impact they can potentially have on your bottom line should serve you well. As noted above, some can be rehabilitated by including additional relevant information, some can be used (sparingly) in particular situations while others should be deleted from your billing vocabulary altogether.

Chapter 4

ADMINISTRATIVE AND CLERICAL WORK

Do Not Pass Go.
Do Not Collect
(<u>insert your hourly fee here</u>).

The content contained in this chapter is by far the most difficult and frustrating for me to relate to you.

Why is that you ask? Because the message I have to share with you is by and large not a good one. Not when it comes to getting paid, anyway. And remember, *that* is our goal here.

One might argue that **everything** you do in furtherance of your client's case should be billable. I mean, if it had to be done then it has to have value, and the client benefitted from the value of that effort, right? I can't argue with you there, but that's not the way this works.

That said, after I give you the bad news about all the things you most likely will never be paid for, where possible, I'm going to highlight situations which you *should* be paid and still others where you *might* be paid. All is not lost.

A. Administrative Tasks

Administrative tasks generally involve the day-to-day functions in the administration and management of a law firm. These tasks are considered part of the firm's overhead expenses and, as such, are properly included within the firm's pricing in the establishment of hourly rates for professional services. Like clerical work (see below), firm administrative tasks may be necessary for the firm to function; however, they are not legal in nature, require no legal experience or acumen, and therefore do not constitute legal work for which the firm may bill a client or fee-paying party.

Administrative tasks commonly include the following:
- Conflict checks
- Assigning work within the firm
- Supervision of firm personnel
- Scheduling meetings, depositions, etc.
- Firm invoice preparation and review
- Reviewing/processing external vendor invoices
- Making travel arrangements
- Arranging court reporters
- Training and education

- Preparing a budget
- Preparing Pro Hac Vice motions/pleadings
- Responding to client auditor reports or requests
- Staffing tasks
- Routine file status reviews
- Filing documents with the court or administrative agencies
- Contacting court clerks (checking the status of filings or dockets)
- Maintaining a calendar or diary
- Tracking the status of records requests, subpoenas, discovery, etc.
- File closing tasks

All this is part of the business of running a practice, but it isn't your client's cost. When an auditor characterizes a time entry as an administrative task it means that you are billing the client for YOUR cost of doing business, not THEIR cost of doing business with you.

So you say you're a lawyer. Then you must bill like one.

Are you:

Going to walk down to the courthouse and file a document? Messenger.

Serving a document? Process server.

Maintaining your calendar? Docket clerk.

Transcribing a document from Spanish/Polish/Lithuanian/Mongolian? Translator.

Bates labeling? Paralegal.

Standing at a file cabinet and pulling a pleading to review? File clerk.

Proofreading? Word processor.

Booking that flight to Boston? Travel agent.

You get my point. These tasks aren't lawyering. Your clients hired you because of your reputation and your legal expertise, not your ability to run the fax machine.

However, let's see what, if anything can be done in order to move any of these and other similar activities from the no-pay administrative bucket to a paid legal task.

Write this:

Meet with associate regarding needed research as well as strategy to rebut plaintiff's claims.

Don't write this:

Meet with associate regarding research assignment.

Why? With regard to in-firm conferences, the focus should always be on leveraging the knowledge of the senior attorney to the junior attorney's benefit, as opposed to a purely assignment-based conversation (e.g., "Go do x or y").

Write this:

> Conference call with opposing counsel scheduling his client's deposition and discussing the status of their overdue discovery responses.

Don't write this:

> Conference call with opposing counsel scheduling his client's deposition.

Why? Your secretary can view your calendar and schedule the deposition but he or she can't discuss the discovery responses (well, maybe they can, but your client wouldn't have that expectation). So, when it comes to communications of this nature, if you have anything substantive to discuss, now is the time to do it. The auditor will have to give you that one.

Write this:

> Forward proposed Settlement Agreement to partner (L. Randall) with my suggestions for revision.

Don't write this:

> Forward proposed Settlement Agreement to partner (L. Randall).

Why? In general, you're not getting anything for forwarding documents internally. This is why, whenever possible, you want to include a substantive comment which frames the communication to a legal task versus an administrative one. I suspect this occurs in many instances, but if you don't state it no one will assume so.

Write this:

Revised Motion for New Trial.

Don't write this:

Proofread Motion for New Trial.

Why? Obviously, you need not be an attorney to proofread a document for grammar purposes. While you may be doing that, I strongly suspect that some degree of revision is taking place. If ANY revision takes place you need to toss the proofreading description overboard and simply focus on the revision aspect — that's what will make all the difference.

Other Situations

Do you need a translator? That will be a cost for your client and translators are not cheap. When possible, have someone on your staff do the job for essentially the same cost. Your client will have no objection to that, and you get to keep more work in-firm.

Do you anticipate an issue with a court filing? There may be perfectly good reasons why your court runner shouldn't file a particular pleading, motion, etc. State why it was necessary to have an attorney or paralegal do so, and you should be fine.

Do you have an out-of-town witness that you need to schedule? Scheduling may involve more than comparing calendars. Your explanation as to the matter at hand and how that impacts the witness and his/her obligations may require your involvement. If it does, then by all means say so.

Searching for or fetching a document from either an online file or a file cabinet will not be billable. But if for whatever reason it takes you 15 minutes and delegating the task was not an option then say so (e.g., "At the request of the client, immediately searched for and obtained _____ and forwarded to him."). It's important to note that auditors are, in general, deferential to client requests, especially in urgent situations.

As I hope you can see, there are many situations in which what may not typically be considered to be a billable task can, in fact, be one. Always be thinking in terms of whether or not your efforts were required. If they were, you may need to state why, but it could be well worth your time to do so.

B. Clerical Tasks

Clerical tasks are not legal in nature, require no legal experience or acumen, and are more appropriately handled by secretarial or other non-billing adjunct firm staff. When a client engages an attorney to provide professional services for an hourly fee, the client should also not be charged for items which are traditionally included in the law firm's *overhead,* such as secretary salaries, costs of maintaining a law library, malpractice insurance, utilities and the like. The billing by attorneys and paralegals for the performance of clerical or secretarial tasks is both unreasonable and inappropriate.

Clerical tasks commonly include the following:
- Printing documents
- Scanning documents

- Organizing documents
- Labeling documents
- Creating case binders
- Updating and making lists
- Searching for documents
- Downloading or uploading documents
- File organization
- Logging/documenting receipt of documents
- Researching addresses or other contact information
- Transcription of documents
- Pickup or delivery of documents
- Obtaining tax identification numbers
- Drafting basic forms such as Certificates of Service

Both administrative work and clerical work share the same common theme — your clients don't want to pay you for doing **any** of it. While that reality may be antithetical to the goal of this book, my job here is to identify situations in which the opposite is or might be true. This of course depends upon the *actual* work performed by you.

Compensation for the tasks listed above (not comprehensive) will in most instances result in a denial of fees sought. Your objective then is to (1) find situations in which *more* was involved and (2) describe that work sufficiently enough to remove it from the not-paid bucket to the paid bucket.

For example, billing for "Receipt of contents of file" won't get you paid. However, by making sure at least some substantive review takes place, it changes the character of the entry: "Receipt of client file and begin detailed review of same in preparation for preparing Answer to Complaint."

Consider a task such as preparing a deposition or trial binder. More often than not, you'll see this work adjusted as a clerical task. And maybe for the most part it is. However, the choice of documents to include may not be suitable for a secretary to undertake. If the task includes tabbing or highlighting documents that have particular relevance, then in my mind the nature of the task has changed. Is legal acumen required? The more the better and that's what your entry should emphasize. For example, "Reviewed file and evaluated relevant documents to include and highlight in trial binder." Emphasizing the analysis aspect of the entry suggests much more than a clerical undertaking and therefore frames the work in the best position to be considered compensable.

In general, time billed for any file organization tasks will be denied. Instead, consider billing for "drafting a comprehensive list of file contents." That task could be performed concurrently with the actual file organization while focusing on a more substantive activity. No doubt you've also had situations where your client appeared to have tossed everything into a bankers box (maybe even several of them), leaving you to sort out the mess. It would not be unreasonable to bring that issue up to them and ask for permission to bill a reasonable amount of time to sort everything out in a usable fashion.

Which brings me to a very important point when facing the need to perform clerical and administrative tasks while not having to write off all of your efforts; If, because of no fault of the firm, you have to engage in any extra effort or perform work you would not otherwise have to do it is reasonable to ask the client to compensate you for that effort, even if it would normally be an unpaid task.

You have to be judicious in choosing your battles, but if you do so under reasonable circumstances and are not demanding in your request for the accommodation, then there is a very good chance the client will respond in a favorable way.

When your client truly values your firm and what it brings to the table, the client will carve out exceptions for tasks other firms will not get paid for. I've witnessed this time and time again and can attest to the fact it works.

And the list of exceptions I've seen is a long one to be sure: uploading and downloading documents from a client server (ostensibly due to the volume of documents involved); Bates stamping documents (again, due to volume of same involved); maintaining a case calendar (due to multiple related client cases); translating documents (when cost to have this done externally is roughly the same); other technical (e.g. computer-related) tasks which are necessitated due to the nature or size of the case.

The possibilities are only limited by your persuasiveness to make the case that the work should be billable due to the circumstances involved. Obviously though, it's all about framing such a request in a way that shows you have your clients' best interest in mind. The fact that it also happens to benefit you and your firm is a bonus.

The beauty of this is that as long as you don't abuse the accommodation it can open the door for other exceptions in the future.

Key Tactics for Administrative and Clerical tasks:

Accept that many of these tasks will simply not be billable. In that case, delegate as much as possible to non-billing firm staff.

If your firm can perform work which would otherwise be farmed out to an external vendor (e.g., translation), then by all means offer the service. They probably won't pay your partner billable rate but they may pay at an associate or paralegal rate.

Take advantage of opportunities to incorporate substantive work to an otherwise non-billable task (e.g., substantive discussion added to an administrative scheduling call).

Leverage atypical situations or client requests which require your involvement in order to change a non-billable activity to a billable one. And make sure your time entry reflects that (e.g., "Task performed by attorney due to _____" or "task performed by attorney per client request to do so.")

If, in your judgment, the matter at hand calls for a special accommodation regarding an otherwise

non-billable task(s), then by all means present that to the client. You'd be amazed how receptive they can be to a reasonable request of this nature. And, if you don't take advantage of that opportunity you'll likely find a receptive ear in the future when circumstances call for another exception.

Chapter 5

FORMULAS FOR DISASTER

Billing on Autopilot

Humans are creatures of habit. Lawyers — although a goodly portion of the population may consider us less than human — are no less disposed to habits. Maybe more so. And sometimes bad ones at that. How we bill our clients often reflects that reality.

While you may think that you haven't picked up any of those bad habits with regard to billing, chances are you have. Among other things, legal auditors are looking for patterns, and we do find them, more often than you'd think. Modern billing software allows us to drill down to the individual level and view your time entries in isolation. Over a month. Many months. A year or multiple years, and over multiple matters. There's probably not a single attorney or paralegal for whom I cannot find some kind of billing pattern when viewing their work in isolation. Many times, those patterns will reveal something that gives the auditor ammunition to reduce your bill.

Since you might not even be aware that a problem exists, it's important to examine some of the common issues found by legal auditors in this area, and then look at solutions for you to eliminate — or at the very least, reduce — the problem as much as possible.

So what is Autopilot Billing? Autopilot Billing refers to repetitive narratives as well as time increments which don't follow logical sequencing, lack proportion to other work performed, or appear to be excessive, premature or unnecessary at a given point in the case.

Below are some of the most common categories (and examples) of what I refer to as Autopilot Billing. Ask yourself if you recognize any of these issues with your own billing.

A. Reflexive Billing

It bears repeating because it applies not only to the issues presented in this subsection, but to almost every issue discussed in this book, that your time will likely be scrutinized by a legal auditor in isolation.

My personal method is to review each timekeeper individually before reviewing the bill in chronological order with all timekeepers. What am I looking for? Well, before anything else, I'm looking to see what your role in the matter is. Aside from that I'm looking for things like repetitive narrative descriptions as well as repetitive time increments billed. Viewed in isolation, issues often immediately jump off my computer screen.

Certain formulaic verbiage becomes readily apparent: For example, attorney Lewis ends most of her time entries with the phrase "and prepared memo to the file re: same." Disregarding block billing considerations created by a tag line such as this (See Chapter 1), doing so can create the appearance of a reflexive and therefore potentially inaccurate time entry. Canned ham, if you will.

Does a memo to the file really need its own memo to the file? Apparently some attorneys think so. Sound ridiculous? Well, it happens. Attorney Lewis also ends many of her time entries with the phrase "and mark trial calendar." Viewed in the extreme, any task or communication may ultimately affect your trial calendar. However, doing so repetitively only makes it appear suspect and included for the purpose of "puffing up" the time you are billing.

That said, I have no doubt that many attorneys have simply gotten into some bad habits and aren't carefully thinking through what they are writing.

A common reflexive description I see is when a lawyer starts every sentence with, "Legal analysis of_____." That's like my doctor billing for "medical analysis of _____" or my local garage billing for "mechanics analysis of _____." That's why your client went to *you*, as opposed to say, their personal trainer. It's nothing more than unnecessary verbiage and it certainly won't immunize the rest of your time entry for what comes next (e.g., "Legal analysis of court reporter invoice."). Unfortunately, that won't help.

Another all-too-common example occurs when the lawyer ends each sentence with the phrase: "and do so in accordance with defense efforts." Which begs the question – Isn't every task you perform done so "in accordance with defense efforts"? Since that's obviously the case, why include an unnecessary phrase such as this in your time entry description? It's not adding value or helping your cause. Quite the contrary, it makes it look like you're attempting to elevate a task that is not billable. **Example:** "Print Motion for New Trial and do so in accordance with defense efforts." More like "and do so in accordance with defense efforts *to get paid*."

Description is one thing. The actual amount of time you bill is the other component and one that can be even more problematic, because it can call into question the accuracy of virtually everything you do.

Example:

> 09/13 Research California case law on tortious interference with contract.   2.70 hours
>
> 09/14 Continued research on CA case law on tortious inference with contract.   2.70 hours
>
> 09/15 Continued research on CA case law on tortious inference with contract.   2.70 hours
>
> 09/16 Completed research on CA case law on tortious inference with contract.   2.70 hours

Hmmmm ... four entries for legal research and all of them are billed at 2.70 hours? Coincidence? Possibly. But chances are, you just like that number. And an examination of your previous months' billing reveals that to be the case. Doesn't mean it's incorrect; however, it does create a red flag which *suggests* a problem.

Ethical billing is, above all, about honesty and accuracy. Guesswork, approximation and/or any form of billing intentionally or unintentionally based on what you habitually bill is unacceptable. To the extent that your billing appears to resemble any of that, you can count on being challenged. The attorneys who get paid *in full* for their work do not set off these kinds of alarm bells. Their entries blend and virtually get lost in the firm's invoice because of the problems that other firm members have. They literally put me to sleep.

This runs counter to the actual practice of law, where you are constantly advocating in order to achieve the desired result for your client. With billing, it's the opposite.

Success = Not getting noticed.

Success = Not standing out.

You're boring and you blend in. Totally unremarkable. When it comes to successful billing, that's the legal professional you want to be. Why? Because it pays!

Review your time entries *before* the bill goes out and take a serious look for patterns. You may be surprised at what you see. Your billing is equivalent to a fingerprint. Each is unique. But remember, getting paid isn't about being unique in our context. It's about being forgettable.

B. "Spread" Billing: 1 + 1 Does Not Equal 2

This billing infraction appears in several situations.

Let's say that you draft a brief letter in which you are confirming to multiple parties that the mediation will take place on October 3. The letter to each party is nearly identical. Are you going to bill three entries at 0.10 hours each or only one? You know the correct answer. If you draft one communication, don't bill for it multiple times if the only difference is that the communication is going to a different party. Your client is only paying you for drafting the first document — that's it.

Want to avoid that result? Even if it's only one sentence, add something *substantive* that would differentiate the letters from one another.
Example:

> 1) Draft letter to plaintiff's attorney confirming that mediation is set for October 3.
>
> 2) Draft letter to Co-Defendant's attorney confirming that mediation is set for October 3, and also discussing planning conference to prepare for same.
>
> 3) Draft letter to client advising that mediation has been set for October 3, and also discussing strategy for same.

Now, I'm not advising that you toss in just anything here, but I am saying that to leave something out could be costly to you. Yes, it's a little more work, but by simply adding an extra sentence or a few more words you're now going to get paid for each and every communication.

Another variation of spread-billing is illustrated by the example below:

03/14 Review Notice of Deposition of C. White.

0.10 hours

03/14 Review Notice of Deposition of K. Mitchell.

0.10 hours

03/14 Review Notice of Deposition of D. Sanders.

0.10 hours

03/14 Review Notice of Deposition of S. Jackson.

0.10 hours

So, you say, "What's wrong with this? I should get a tenth of an hour for reviewing each notice. That's fair, isn't it?" Well, yes, it would be, except for the small detail that it didn't take you 16 – 24 minutes to read all four notices. Assuming no document production requests, six minutes or less would have been plenty of time to review all of them.

Yet, on an almost daily basis I see this happen. And many times it's even uglier. It's not uncommon to see an attorney bill 2 hours for reviewing 20 subpoenas. I'm referring to 20 separate entries at 0.10 hours for each. All those entries may look impressive on your bill, but an auditor is likely going to know better. If I was jaded, I might imagine the attorney's eyes light up when he received those 20 subpoenas — "Yeah baby, I got an extra hour for lunch today!" Okay, maybe I am jaded, if only because I witness these opportunists on a regular basis.

"Wait a minute," you say, "what the heck is this guy supposed to do? Back in Chapter 1 you made it clear that multiple tasks should be separately billed." And you'd have a point were if not for the following **exception:** multiple tasks should be billed separately *unless they would result in an inflation of the time spent.*

In our 20 subpoena example, billing separately would result in an inflation of the time spent (and therefore billed).

In this scenario the auditor will generally employ something like a 3 to 1 ratio to adjust the time billed. You'd get a tenth of an hour credit for every 3 similar notices or form documents you review. So, Mr. Extended Lunch would get seven-tenths of an hour (0.70) for reviewing the 20 subpoenas in our example. Fair? You be the judge. However, it's rarely if ever that attorneys appeal this particular adjustment.

Let's suppose you billed 1.40 hours for reviewing all 20 subpoenas. In that case it's unlikely that any adjustment would occur because it appears that the attorney is exercising billing judgment by not squeezing out a tenth of an hour for each document.

So what's the lesson here? Look, if it took you exactly 2 hours I'm not telling you not to bill that. What I am telling you is that you should be aware that alarm bells go off if you bill in what *appears* to be a formulaic way.

Yet another variation on this scenario occurs when the attorney is reviewing multiple notices or other form documents prepared by paralegal or support staff. Another 20 subpoenas and another 2 hours billed to "review, revise and execute subpoena to ABC Hospital" — followed by another 19 entries with the same description to other providers.

Think about the language of this time entry — "review" — "revise" — "execute". You had to revise all 20 subpoenas? Are you kidding me? If you're not, then your paralegal's ability may be suspect, to say the least. And your client isn't going to pay you for revising *everything* you or another timekeeper does, either. "Execute"? An impressive word and someone may think you're doing something very lawyerly here, but the auditor won't be impressed. Even if you're a stickler on good penmanship, we're talking about only a matter of seconds to sign your name.

The point is that billing like this looks formulaic and downright opportunistic — it's poison. Give the auditor something to work with. If you had to revise 8 of the 20 subpoenas tell them that. It would be hard to argue that you were following any discernible formula by doing so.

C. Unit Billing: Billing by the Numbers

So what do I mean by Unit Billing? Client Billing Guidelines almost universally mandate that services should be for the *actual* time spent on any task using units of one-tenth (0.10) of an hour and that a firm may not round time to units greater than one-tenth. Like reflexive billing and spread-billing, it's the (apparent) failure to precisely bill the actual time spent performing a given task which is at issue here. The issue most often manifests itself when attorneys bill predominately in whole and half-hour time increments.

FORMULAS FOR DISASTER

For example, when viewed in isolation, the auditor observes that the attorney has 50 entries over the course of a month and 45 of those entries amazingly took exactly 0.5, 1.0, 1.5, 2.0, 2.5, 3.0, etc., to accomplish. If not for a handful of tasks under 0.5 hours, each and every entry above that or close to it *happened* to take that long to accomplish.

No, I am not a statistician. However, I really don't need to be one to know that something is wrong with this picture. A review of prior months and even years' worth of billing by this attorney will nearly always confirm that the attorney billed using the same method. Anecdotally, I can state that I've never had an attorney challenge me when this specific issue has arisen. Given that most attorneys are willing to engage in a certain amount of battle over reductions to their bills, I see this as quite telling.

Subsequent billing (post adjustment) by the attorney generally takes several forms. Aside from not changing his billing behavior or not correcting the problem, often an intermediate step occurs. All of a sudden his bills are plagued by time ending in "4" or "9" (e.g., 1.4, 1.9, 2.4, 2.9, 3.4, etc.). It has become a rarity that his time ends precisely on the hour or half hour. His new method is simply to drop the rounded time by a tenth of an hour. This becomes as obvious as if he were still billing precisely on the hour or half-hour.

Guesswork or estimation of your time is not only unacceptable, it's unethical. I will continue to pound the drum-beat: Bill your client for how long it took you to perform the task. No more and no less. The numbers will magically appear natural (e.g., 0.6, 1.0, 2.3, 3.7, 4.5, etc.)...you get the picture.

Getting Paid

Another version of unit billing is doing so by task. Let's take a quick look at "Joe." Joe Lawyer works hard for his dollar but hasn't forgotten that he is no longer working on the assembly line. In June, Joe billed time to draft an Answer. Joe worked hard on that Answer and billed the client 2.3 hours. Joe's been doing good work and the client has passed four other new matters to him this month. At the end of the month Joe bills his other new matters. Yeah, you guessed it. Four Answers drafted at exactly 2.3 hours each.

As you now know, the auditor is looking for patterns and Joe has given one with a mighty red flag attached. Now *all* of Joe's time becomes suspect. The auditor can reasonably conclude that Joe didn't spend precisely 2.3 hours on each Answer.

I know this may sound like a broken record but your numbers tell a story. I see lawyers every day who have gotten in the habit of *billing the same amount of time for every similar task they engage in.*

Example:

    Draft Defendant's Interrogatories to Plaintiff.   1.00 hours

    Draft Defendant's Request for Production to Plaintiff.
                                                           0.80 hours

    Draft Defendant's Request for Disclosure to Plaintiff.
                                                           0.50 hours

Nothing wrong here, except that as sure as the sun rises in the East, this guy will bill the **same** amount of time for every similar task on every case. Let's be honest, it should not take the same amount of time for the same task on each case. If an auditor observes this (and sooner or later they will), your corresponding time entries will be subject to adjustments. And, like it or not, they'll probably conclude that it took you less time. I mean, why wouldn't you bill more if it actually took longer?

Attorneys routinely respond by stating that the amount billed was "the *average* amount of time" they spent on the task. This answer never ceases to amaze me. Where did you get the idea that averaging the amount of time it took you to accomplish a given task was an acceptable form of billing?

The message here is a simple one — bill **exactly** the amount of time it took you to do the work. If for some reason you want to *write down* your time then by all means do so, but please don't get in the habit of arbitrarily assigning a certain amount of time for a given task. If the auditor is doing his job it will eventually come back to cost you...guaranteed.

D. Disjointed/Fragmented Billing To be continued...

Yes, I understand that Rome was not built in a day. However, I see some attorneys who can't seem to draft any substantive document or report in the same day. The following day or a couple of days later they pick up the ball and start running with it again.

Example 1:

> 11/01 Conduct detailed review of file in preparation for drafting comprehensive status report to client.   2.20 hours

> 11/01 Began drafting comprehensive status report to client.
> 1.40 hours
>
> 11/10 Continue drafting comprehensive status report to client.
> 1.10 hours
>
> 11/15 Complete comprehensive status report to client.
> 1.80 hours

I get it. Devoting seven hours to the same task in one day may not be feasible. You have many clients and it wasn't possible for you to complete the work that day. However, the problem arises when the task gets stretched out over multiple days or weeks with large gaps in between. Doing so seems inefficient, and could cause more time to be expended because of all the starting and stopping involved.

Example 2:

> 11/01 Detailed review of file in order to begin drafting comprehensive status report to client. 2.20 hours
>
> 11/01 Began drafting comprehensive status report to client.
> 1.40 hours
>
> 11/21 Continued detailed review of file in order to continue drafting comprehensive status report to client. 1.10 hours
>
> 12/02 Completed drafting comprehensive status report to client. 2.90 hours

The problem is compounded as in the above example whenever the dates between working on the task appear further and further apart. If you are writing that client report on November 1 and three weeks go by before you touch the file again to work on it, and same is accompanied by time billed for additional file review, that is a problem. If there is a reason for the time delay then try to incorporate that into your entry (e.g., "Delay in completing report due to several weeks in trial."). At the very least, explain the need for the additional file review: "Performed additional file review in order to update client on plaintiff's recent settlement offer." Make sure a trail appears on your invoice showing these recent events (e.g., "Telephone conference with plaintiff's counsel regarding settlement offer.") in order to show that the need was real and not some kind of refresher caused by your own avoidable delay.

Example 3:

05/10 Reviewed proposed settlement agreement from plaintiff's attorney.   0.40 hours

05/10 Conference call with plaintiff's attorney resulting in settlement of matter.   0.90 hours

05/10 Drafted Stipulation of Dismissal.   0.10 hours

05/10 Drafted monthly status report to client informing of settlement including strategy for continued defense of this matter.   0.50 hours

06/05 Received file-stamped copy of Stipulation of Dismissal.   0.10 hours

06/10 Drafted monthly status report to client including strategy for continued defense of this matter.   0.50 hours

In the above example, the attorney typically ends his monthly client report time entries with the tag: "for continued defense of this matter." Ignoring that tag-line (addressed earlier), the case had been settled weeks before and the client was informed of this fact. The only thing left to do before closing out the matter was waiting for the court to send a stamped copy of the Stipulation and Order of Dismissal. Yet, like clockwork, because he religiously sends the client a report every 30 days, the attorney bills 0.50 hours for "drafting updated status report to client," including developing "strategy for continued defense of this matter." There is no apparent need to develop a strategy for the continued defense of this matter as it is over for all practical purposes. Nor should any strategy be necessary to wait on a Stipulation of Discontinuance. Billing on *autopilot* is never a good thing.

It's my observation that upon the conclusion of the matter many attorneys become a bit lax in their billing, even if they've been stellar throughout the case. You don't want to tarnish your fine work by being careless at the end.

Let's take a look at another variation of the problem.

Example 4:

05/10 Review of file in order to prepare monthly status report to client.　　　　　　　　　　　　　　　0.40 hours

05/10 Prepare monthly client status report.　　0.50 hours

06/08 Review of file in order to prepare monthly status report to client.　　　　　　　　　　　　　　　0.40 hours

06/08 Prepare monthly client status report.　　0.50 hours

There's one big issue here. According to your bill, nothing happened between 5/10 and 6/08. Your invoice does not include any entries between those dates evidencing that anything occurred. Given that, how could the 6/08 entry for preparing the monthly status report possibly take 0.50 hours to prepare? And how could the file review take 0.40 hours to accomplish if nothing happened in the interim between the last monthly report?

If little or nothing happened in those interim weeks, that's a potential problem. It appears that you're cruising along on autopilot. In the absence of nothing new to report, each of those tasks shouldn't have taken longer than 0.10 or 0.20 hours unless you have something new to address. If you do, then make it clear what that is, especially if your time entries indicate that little or nothing occurred in the interim. It's also possible that events did in fact transpire, but for some good reason they were deemed to be non-billable tasks. That's another reason I recommend that your final bill includes time written off by the firm. It may not be part of the *billable* story your invoice tells, but it's nonetheless a part of the story. Always err on the side of inclusiveness.

E. The "Desert Island" Time Entry

The examples go something like this:

Example 1:

> File review regarding the status of depositions to determine what depositions need to be scheduled.

Example 2:

> File review of medical records to determine what records still need to be obtained.

At first glance all of these would appear to be acceptable entries with no issues. So what's wrong? In all examples, the entries are stand-alone. That is, no other work was performed which was related to the tasks undertaken.

In Example 1, no depositions were identified or scheduled. In Example 2, no medical records were identified as needed or ordered. Both concern tasks performed in which the reader would anticipate seeing additional related work (e.g., the scheduling of depositions and the ordering of additional medical records). Well, you say, "Maybe the attorney decided no other depositions were needed and no other records were necessary." Fair enough. But be aware that these kind of stand-alone status-related entries give the appearance that the biller wanted to invoice some time to the file. Obviously, you want to avoid that.

To get off the Desert Island, make it clear that as a result of the review you decided to do or not do something, as in the revised examples below.

> Brief review of medical records received to date and concluded that no additional records are needed at this time.

> Reviewed the status of this matter and determined that no additional depositions are warranted at this time.

An outcome should always be apparent. By adding the additional details the results of the review are now clear and unambiguous. The necessity of the task is now not in question.

Example 3:

> Periodic review of client file in order to prepare updated status report.

Example 4:

> Conducted comprehensive review of file in order to prepare for plaintiff's deposition.

Examples 3 and 4 (above) go a step further and describe tasks in which additional related work is not merely suggested but *expected*.

If you billed time to review the file in order to draft a status report, there should be a corresponding time entry evidencing that you did exactly that. Likewise, if you conducted a file review to prepare for a deposition the reviewer will expect to see an entry in which that occurred. Again, circumstances could arise which would make both tasks unnecessary (e.g., the case unexpectedly settled after the review). In that case the *story* contained in your invoices should leave no doubt as to what transpired.

F. Timing of Work Performed: Is there something wrong with my calendar?

Yes, the right hand should know what the left hand is doing, but sometimes doesn't. And the cart shouldn't be before the horse.

What do these two old sayings have in common with legal bills? Nothing, other than they apply with a frequency that is unacceptable. As discussed, your bill is another chapter in the story of the matter you are handling. One lousy chapter can ruin an otherwise fine book. Since your bill isn't fiction, it had better make sense.

Take a look at the following and ask yourself if the story makes sense.

Example 1:

06/17 Draft Defendant's Answer and Counterclaim to Plaintiff's Complaint.

06/18 Filed Defendant's Answer and Counterclaim to Plaintiff's Complaint.

06/22 Reviewed our Answer and Counterclaim for accuracy and completeness.

Pay attention — wouldn't you review the Answer and Counterclaim *before* you filed them?

Example 2:

05/03 Paralegal discusses cancellation of plaintiff's deposition on 5/07 with opposing counsel.

05/06 Associate prepares for plaintiff's deposition.

05/07 (As expected) no deposition occurs.

Stuff happens. Perhaps the associate didn't get the word on the cancellation. Regardless, your client doesn't have to pay for the firm's failure to communicate.

Example 3:

09/01 Associate receives and reviews new file from client, drafts an Answer and then advises the client of same (without block billing…of course).

09/12 Partner receives new file and sends acknowledgement letter to the client thanking her for the assignment.

Considering that your client has already been advised by your firm that you have received the file and drafted and filed an Answer, ask yourself what does this add other than making it appear you are communicating a redundant message? Additionally, and as an aside: Never bill simply for receiving anything. If you must, then give it a no-charge unless you also reviewed whatever it was that you received. Obviously, no legal knowledge is required in order to relate that you received a file from the mailroom. Also, absent substantive commentary, take the same approach with regard to any acknowledgement letter. Write it and either no-charge it or keep it off your bill if it's only to relate that you received the file.

Example 4:

Settlement is generally a good thing, but in my world odd things seem to happen in the closing phase of the case.

3/10 On this date the matter settled and the partner sent a closing letter to the client.

End of story? No, I'm afraid we're not done yet...

3/22 Review of file to determine upcoming discovery deadlines to aid in preparation of case strategy.

The reason for the above example that I most often read on appeal is that the timekeeper's actual entry was inadvertently entered on the wrong date. This is a shame because the error should be quite easy to spot and correct. In a much smaller amount of cases one timekeeper is simply not on the same page with everyone else and actually performs tasks after the case has concluded. An accounting mistake is going to happen once in a while but that kind of error really shouldn't occur at all.

Example 5:

6/11 Write closing letter to the client.

Pretty much by definition we are assuming that the matter is completely wrapped-up when this final communication goes out to the client. But no, more than two months later:

8/18 Finalize closing letter to the client.

Certainly some event or issue must have transpired which would cause such a delay, you say. Not according to the time entries on the bill. The August 18 entry appears directly underneath the June 11 entry. Okay, well maybe something happened and it wasn't recorded as an entry. It could have, but then again the final correspondence description offers no information as to why it took over two months to finalize the letter.

Taking into account the fact that your bill is like a short story, assume that the beginning and the ending may well receive a higher degree of scrutiny, especially the ending. Don't flub your masterpiece with an ending that would have Quentin Tarantino scratching his head. While your bill is neither pulp nor fiction, it may yet end in a similarly unpleasant fashion.

G. Preparation for Trial, Hearings and Depositions: Rome wasn't built in half a day

For some reason, maybe an unwritten law that I'm not privy to, an enormous amount of cases are settled late in the day. I mean, when they say cases settle on the eve of trial they really mean *eve of trial*! You prepare extensively for trial and late in the day your 8 hours of trial prep are wiped out by a 0.30 hour call resulting in settlement. This is completely understandable for many reasons we don't need to discuss here.

However, this seems to happen more with some attorneys than others and I'm not only talking about settlement on the eve of trial.

I'm referring to extensive preparation for hearings and depositions which are cancelled. I've noticed patterns with particular attorneys where this happens on a fairly regular basis. For them, nothing is ever settled or cancelled at noon. Why not? Because they'd like to bill another 5 hours on this file today? Of course YOU would never do such a thing. That said, I want to help you to avoid the inadvertent *appearance* of any issue in this area. See the examples below to ensure no question of this nature arises.

Example 1:

> 10/01 Conduct extensive preparation for trial by reviewing and editing outlines for plaintiff and all witnesses (case settled at 4:37 p.m.)   7.30 hours

Example 2:

12/12 Prepared for Plaintiff's deposition by reviewing all discovery responses and editing outline (afternoon deposition cancelled at last minute due to plaintiff's illness).

3.90 hours

Example 3:

01/07 Prepared for hearing on Motion for Summary Judgment by reviewing our motion and plaintiff's reply motion (afternoon hearing postponed due to judge's illness).

3.60 hours

By adding the details in parenthesis you provide the auditor with important information that resolves any doubt about the circumstances. I can assure you that your effort in doing so will be appreciated. It's a win-win for all concerned.

I. Déjà Vu – Haven't we seen this picture before?

Closely related to the above situation is the problem that occurs when the deposition, hearing or trial is cancelled or postponed and then rescheduled, and preparation is undertaken again. For the auditor, the key question is: "should the time spent in preparation the second time around take as much time as it did when the attorney initially prepared for the event?"

It bears repeating that the auditor will generally tread carefully in relation to evaluating how much time is *too much* time? However, at some point the details call out for taking some kind of action.

<u>Two questions arise:</u>

1) How much or how little time occurred between events?

2) How much or how little happened in the case between events?

Example 1:

01/04 Conducted extensive preparation for trial by reviewing and editing outlines for plaintiff and all witnesses for trial on 1/05 (case postponed)   7.80 hours

01/12 Engaged in extensive preparation for trial by reviewing and editing outlines for plaintiff and all witnesses.
                                                                                        7.60 hours

01/13 Trial Day 1   7.90 hours

Assuming that little if anything substantive happened in the week between the postponed trial and the new date, is it reasonable that the preparation time billed was virtually the same on both dates?

For the most part I would say the answer is "No." While some time in preparation would certainly be expected, absent new events in the interim, a full day of preparation a week later appears excessive.

Let's say that the attorney became aware of a new witness and was successful in quickly deposing him/her, and further that the facts uncovered significantly affected the case. Okay, I'm reaching here to be sure. The point is that if new developments occur in the interim, the attorney's time entries should reflect same and thus inform the auditor of those facts, thereby minimizing or eliminating any concern over the trial preparation time billed the second time around.

When larger spans of time occur between the original and re-scheduled event *the concern by the auditor tends to significantly lessen.*

Example 2:

10/01 Conduct extensive preparation for trial by reviewing and editing outlines for plaintiff and all witnesses (trial postponed at 4:37 p.m.)   7.30 hours

01/16 Conduct extensive preparation for trial by reviewing and editing outlines for plaintiff and all witnesses
                                                                    7.10 hours

01/17 Trial Day 1   8.30 hours

In this example, two and a half months occurred between trial dates. While on average an attorney may do better than the average person in retaining complex information, it's fair to say no one would expect all of the specific details to be retained for that length of time. Add to this the possibility that new developments could surface in the interim.

Your main concern in this area should be in the situation in which there is a short time between events and little or nothing new happens in the case. If that is the case and you are billing roughly the same amount of time, vary your time entry description to reflect anything new you are doing this time around as opposed to previously. *Always* err on the side or more information.

J. Disproportionality of Time Billed: What's wrong with this picture?

Here, we are referring to situations in which the time billed between two or more tasks and/or events appear disproportionate to one another. Some common scenarios follow:

Example 1:

> 05/05 Reviewed newly-received file in order to draft new matter report to client.   4.40 hours
>
> 05/05 Drafted new matter report to client.   0.30 hours

Does it make sense that a 4+ hour file review would only yield a 0.30 hour new matter report to the client? It doesn't to me.

Example 2:

> 08/14 Attend and conduct deposition of plaintiff. 1.20 hours
>
> 08/14 Draft summary of plaintiff's deposition.   4.90 hours

Look, there is no formula here. It simply comes down to what appears to be a logical result. Yes, the deposition could have been so impactful and chock full of information that it could take almost 5 hours to report on a deposition which lasts barely over an hour. Absent that situation, it would be easy to conclude that the time billed to draft the summary is excessive in relation to the time billed to conduct the deposition. If that's the case, add a bit more information to make it understandable as to why the summary would take that long. By taking less than a minute to add a sentence that makes it clear that you had a lot to say and why and/or that the summary was 10 pages long, you've added critical details clarifying your work and any concerns about same.

Example 3:

> 07/17 Prepared for hearing on Motion to Compel Interrogatory Responses by reviewing all file materials and correspondence to date.   3.10 hours
>
> 07/17 Attend and argued Motion to Compel.   0.70 hours

The reasons for what appears to be excessive preparation may result from a tortured history of difficult communications with opposing counsel. The point here is to be aware of the apparent disproportionality and offer some details to alleviate that concern (e.g.,"...and also reviewed extensive file correspondence evidencing unreasonable demands and contentions by opposing counsel to date.")

As always, a little extra detail can go a long way to resolve any questions.

Example 4:

> 09/21 Conducted detailed review of medical records from XYZ Medical Center.   5.70 hours
>
> 09/22 Drafted chronology of plaintiff's records from XYZ Medical Center.   3.80 hours

Here, proportionality is not so much the question as the lack of details. By simply inserting language in the 9/21 entry to the effect that you reviewed 450 pages of medical records from XYZ Medical Center, questions of proportionality are essentially resolved.

Sadly, attorneys (and paralegals) do themselves a disservice by failing to understand the effect that perceived disproportionality can have on their billing, which in turn can unfortunately result in erroneous adjustments to their work.

By following the above suggestions and becoming more aware of potential perceived disproportionality in your time entries, you can greatly lessen the likelihood that either your client or the auditor will question your work.

The end game is to get paid, in full, and the first time. You do not want to have to argue with the client or their auditors and have to appeal and explain that the conclusions reached are not fair. Who needs *that* nonsense? Not you, my friend.

K. Excessive Time – It took you how long to do that?

If there is one area in which auditors tread delicately, it's in judging how much time it takes to do a particular task. While we do, we do so *very* carefully. Billing guidelines (when in effect) provide some standards, but it's really more of a "Does this pass the smell test?" consideration coupled with our own auditing/legal experience.

While you might think that the focus is always on larger tasks what often stands out are the smaller *de minimas* tasks.

The number 1 is the loneliest number for some attorneys. One-tenth of an hour, that is. 0.10. That's 6 minutes or less.

I'm not sure why, but some attorneys and paralegals appear to not be able to accomplish ANY task in 6 minutes or less. And no, I'm not kidding here. As discussed previously, auditors have software at their disposal allowing them to look back into your billing history. Patterns emerge. An extremely obvious one is the bizarre absence of work billed in anything less than 0.20 hours. That's a huge red flag. It suggests that they are either new to the profession, painfully slow, or worse.

Have you ever reviewed an enclosure letter? Forwarded a document with a one sentence comment? Answered or sent a brief e-mail? Reviewed a hearing notice? Of course you have. But for some attorneys, tenth of an hour (0.10) entries are more rare than Bigfoot sightings.

If you can't accomplish any task in under 6 minutes you have an issue. And it's a much bigger one than you think. In fact, I would submit to you that everything you bill is now under the microscope. Fair? Maybe not. But that's the insidious part of billing in this manner. By *seemingly* fudging the small stuff, everything else becomes highlighted as a potential overcharge.

Every time I see an attorney (or paralegal) bill 0.20 hours or more for reviewing a simple notice or cover letter they could have read in less than a minute I have to shake my head.

In my opinion, the following, if they are even billed at all, should never be billed at more than one-tenth of an hour:

1) Drafting or reviewing cover letters. (Absent substantive discussion).

2) Leaving or listening to voice-mail messages. (The maximum message length is typically 3 minutes).

3) Drafting or reviewing hearing or deposition notices. (Absent document request attachments)

4) Sending acknowledgement communications of any kind.

Aside from these tasks which are on the very low end of the expected time scale, the auditor, as previously mentioned, will tread delicately before questioning time for larger tasks, but they have no choice when things appear out of whack either. At some point the time billed may appear so incongruent from what is expected that the auditor may simply adjust your time and request the document at issue or more details in order to justify what was billed.

Drafting form discovery requests? These can often be generated in only several tenths of an hour. If you're billing two hours it should be clear why it took you that long. The same can be said of standard motions such as a Motion to Compel. It shouldn't take 10 hours, but we all know this is only a generalization.

So what can you do to avoid getting flagged for excessive time?

- Ask yourself, if you knew nothing more than what you wrote in your time entry would that cause you to question the time billed? If you would at all question it, then err of the side of a little more detail clarifying why such should not be the case.
- Dealing with complex or novel issues of law? Then by all means, describe them.

- Is the length of the pleading or motion longer than usual due to these or other factors? If yes, put the number of pages in parenthesis at the end of your entry:

Drafted Motion to Compel (13 pages).   6.30 hours.

Other situations are often less than clear, but reasonableness should always rule the day. For instance, there's no rule regarding how long should you should wait at a no-show deposition. My own general rule is that anything beyond one hour would be excessive. However, one can envision all sorts of scenarios as to why an attorney would or should wait longer. The point is that no one is going to know unless you provide those details. After all, you're waiting anyway.

This advice is applicable to everything we're talking about in this book. It's that important. Whether you have hundreds or maybe even thousands riding on one task, don't short-change yourself by providing the briefest description possible because you can't bill the two minutes it took you to write it. That's the ultimate penny-wise and pound-foolish move.

L. Travel and Time

Not that you would ever do this, but time billed to travel seems to be fodder for the opportunist to "puff up" his/her billable time. If the auditor sees an entry for two hours of travel time to go 40 miles they immediately ask why. Was there a snowstorm in the Northeast? Good idea to mention that fact. How about a 10-car pileup on the interstate that left you going nowhere on the freeway for 3 hours? Absolutely include those details.

FORMULAS FOR DISASTER

The distance between locations can be verified in only seconds by looking up Google Maps or other sources. So unless you're riding a burro or taking a rickshaw to your court appearance, the time billed in relation to the distance covered should be reasonably related.

If you're traveling via airplane, chances are you will also be providing an expense receipt for the trip which includes the actual flight time. Either way, flight time is readily ascertainable and the auditor will often check that via various online flight calculators. You should assume that will be the case with the time you are billing if things appear to be out of whack.

Travel to the airport or train and associated wait times are somewhat murky areas. Billing guidelines often make it clear that the client will only pay for actual time spent in flight or other mode of travel. That means your time getting to the airport or train and waiting for same to disembark may not be paid, although associated expenses (e.g., cab, mileage) are almost always reimbursed.

Some clients will only pay your hourly rate when traveling if you **work** during the flight. If that is the case with your particular client, make sure your time entry makes that fact perfectly clear:

> Travel to Chicago and prepared for plaintiff's deposition by drafting outline during flight.

> Return travel to New York and prepared summary of plaintiff's deposition during flight.

Although this book is not focused on expenses, I would be remiss by not addressing a few points which frequently arise in the travel arena.

If you are operating under client billing guidelines most common expenses will be covered. But even if you're not, you should **observe these considerations**:

- Do not bill for First Class travel.
- Do not bill for luxury hotel accommodations. (You don't have to stay at The Knotty Pine, but The Four Seasons is unnecessary.)
- Do not bill for high end restaurants (While you're not regulated to eating Happy Meals, a 54-ounce porterhouse steak at Ruth's Chris is pushing the limits)
- Skip billing for incidentals such as laundry. It's not the client's fault you have a ketchup stain on that nice, pressed, white oxford.
- And, without a doubt your client's #1 pet peeve: Billing for alcohol. DO NOT do this! I've witnessed relationships sour over this. Unless your client is with you and asks you to bill for that bottle of wine, don't do it.

When it comes to travel expenses, it's one part reasonableness, one part moderation and one part common sense. You got this.

M. Long Billing Days: Burning the Midnight Oil

Face it, attorneys work lots of hours. Long days are a fact of life at most busy firms. However, your client is almost guaranteed to question (or even prohibit) anything over eight or ten *billed* hours in one day absent their approval and you being in trial, engaged in lengthy travel, or facing some significant deadline. If you've put in a long billable day, your time should be as descriptive as necessary to explain why the time was necessary. An auditor will know if you've passed that magic number of 8 or 10 hours or whatever your client's rules are.

Consider the realities of a 10 hour billable day for one matter. Let's say you began work at 9:00 a.m. In order for you to invoice ten hours, you would have to work until 7:00 p.m. without stopping. No bathroom breaks. No personal calls. No office chit-chat. No calls or e-mails with other clients. How realistic does that sound to you? An honest response would say "not very." Lawyers ARE human. It's more likely that you'll be working until 9:00 p.m. to get those 10 billable hours in.

When the number of hours billed in one day ratchets up from there, the same practical realities are present, making extremely long days dubious at best and viewed with a high level of scrutiny. As the court in *Metro Data Systems, Inc. v. Durango Systems, Inc.*, 597 F. Supp. 244, 246 (D. Ariz. 1984) stated, a day in which one lawyer claimed to have worked 18.90 hours is "almost *ipso facto* excessive." Similarly, as the court stated in *Chrapliwy v. Uniroyal, Inc.*, 583 F. Supp. 40, 50 (N.D. Ind.

Getting Paid

1983), "a day with 10 billable hours, while extraordinary, will occasionally occur. But 17 days where billable hours equaled or exceeded 12 hours is not justifiable. A 20 hour day is questionable."

Yet, I've witnessed attorneys and paralegals bill nearly 24 hours in a single day as well as several days at 20+ hours in a row. A Herculean feat to be sure.

The usual answers:

Sorry, I meant to bill 10 of those hours on the next day.

Good answer.

That phone call was supposed to be 0.20 hours, not 20.0 hours.

Yep. Appreciate the attention to detail.

You've never prepared for trial before, have you?

Yes, I have, but one need not be F. Lee Bailey to know that generally even in the absence of sleep, chances are that you're going to take a break at some point, bodily functions being what they are.

And...my all-time favorite:

My flight crossed the International Date Line, so it appeared that it was 24 hours.

No kidding.

I'm reminded of a scene from the movie *The Firm*, where the partner tells Tom Cruise that he should bill whenever he thinks about the case. Basically, as long as he's conscious and can articulate some remotely intelligent reason to bill the client, it's open season to crank the firm's money press.

Okay, these are obviously *extreme* examples and it's definitely not the 1980s anymore (despite the fact that Bon Jovi is still touring). Suffice to say that auditors are well aware of the fact that lawyers work long hours — in fact, we know it so well that it's quite often the reason why a goodly number of us are doing what we are doing and not what you're doing.

But we also understand that the pressure on you to bill is still there. I mean, I *know* lawyers. Even if you crushed it last year, it's often still "What have you done for me lately?" That's frustrating. And to top it off, many of your clients are tightwads who hire folks like me to take your bill and perform the equivalent of a proctology exam on it.

Enter legal auditing software (which is by and large useless). However, one thing it does do well is keeping track of numbers. Your numbers. Your hours. Let's say you have a client called ZXY Insurance Company. The client likes the work your firm does and at any given time you have 40 – 50 open matters with them and you work on about half of those in one capacity or another.

All of those matters (including those you work on) are generally billed monthly. So, for any given month, you may have 20 or more invoices with your time on them. If the client has a prohibition for work over 8 or 10 hours in a single day, the software will flag all of your time for any day in which 8 or 10 hours is exceeded. Therefore, if you work 0.50 hours on average for those 22 matters, the software will "know" you billed 11 hours on that day.

While on one hand, clients will prohibit time in excess of 8 or 10 hours in one day, they also recognize that special situations, as well as trial work, will dictate that flexibility is required on their part to allow you to do the work necessary to successfully handle the matter. Your first order of business then, is to keep your client informed of potential situations in which your time may exceed the rules.

While it's understood that you do not have a crystal ball, to the extent you can identify events and possible dates or time periods when longer days may be required, the better off you will be. Make no mistake, it's not so much that your client has anything against long days or giving you approval for same; it's that they don't like surprises. Particularly surprises in the form of unexpectedly larger invoices.

One important caveat of note: Client approval regarding long billing days does not provide immunity for other billing issues. All it means is that you can bill beyond the daily maximum number of hours. That's it. Start block-billing or having the partner make copies and the ginsu knife of the auditing samurai will no doubt be unsheathed.

Let's suppose, however, that you do not have approval for billing beyond 10 hours or whatever the daily maximum number of hours set by your client. And let's further suppose that late in the day your client wants you to assess and summarize legal precedent on a particular matter you are handling. Doing the research takes your total time for that client over the 12 hour mark for that day.

If you think that's likely, then you should inform the client either right then and there or as soon as it's practical to do so. Your client wanted you to perform the work and will unquestionably approve the time.

Example 1:

09/17 Began draft of Motion for Summary Judgment.
6.60 hours

09/17 Telephone call from and conference with claims representative Wallace regarding research memorandum needed quickly on spoliation issue in Atkinson case.
0.30 hours

09/17 Researched spoliation issue at the request of claim rep Wallace (who approved time over 10 hours on this date).
3.60 hours

09/17 Drafted research memorandum on spoliation issue per request of claim rep Wallace (who approved time over 10 hours on this date).
2.20 hours

The added information in parenthesis is worth its weight in gold to you. Your client and/or their auditor will appreciate the fact that you are attuned to the rules. And while a careful reading of the narratives above should be enough to prevent them from erroneously cutting those hours from your bill, it's added insurance for you.

Yet, in the course of real life things sometimes happen which are totally out of your control. So, if you're driving to a deposition on the other side of the state and you get stuck in a massive traffic jam or a snowstorm which throws you over the daily limit — by all means say so!

Example 2:

> 10/19 Travel by car from Seattle to Spokane to attend plaintiff's deposition. 4.10 hours
>
> 10/19 Took plaintiff's deposition. 2.70 hours
>
> 10/19 Return travel by automobile from plaintiff's deposition in Spokane to Seattle (major accident delay on Highway 90). 6.30 hours

Auditors don't apply rules in a vacuum. Where we can justifiably overlook the rule we'll be happy to do that — give us the ammunition and we'll have your back. But if you don't, it'll appear that you took a detour that day so you could check out a new rod and reel at Bass Pro Shop or took an extra-long lunch. In all seriousness though, whatever the reason, PLEASE err on the side of including the pertinent details of the situation which caused or contributed to the long day.

N. Does anyone really know what time it is?

The answer in far too many cases is a definite "no!" What I'm specifically referring to is exemplified by the problem identified in subheading "F" above but applied to situations occurring on the same date as applied to office conferencing, depositions, hearings and trial in which multiple attorneys are billing to attend the same event. The examples below tell the story.

Example 1:

05/05 Teleconference with client (C. Adams) and partner (J. Thomas) regarding strategy in light of denial of our Motion for Summary Judgment.   1.10 hours
[Associate D. Fowler]

05/05 Teleconference with client (C. Adams) and associate (D. Fowler) regarding strategy in light of denial of our Motion for Summary Judgment.   0.70 hours
[Partner J. Thomas]

Example 2:

06/19 Attend and participate in the deposition of plaintiff.
[Associate D. Fowler]   3.70 hours

06/19 Attend and conduct the deposition of plaintiff.
[Partner J. Thomas]   4.20 hours

Example 3:

12/11 Attend Trial Day 1.   9.50 hours
[Associate D. Fowler]

12/11 Attend Trial Day 1.   8.10 hours
[Partner J. Thomas]

As you can see, the issue is that the amount of time billed to the same event by each attorney is different. One of the attorneys is billing the wrong amount of time. As to which one, it's impossible for the auditor or anyone for that matter to know.

That said, there may be explanations for the incongruity.

In the office conferencing Example 1, let's suppose that the call took place in a conference room and the associate arrived a bit early to prepare. Instead of being precise about the length of the call, he rolled the preparation and call time together. Whatever the reason, it's almost guaranteed that if an auditor spots this he'll cut the associate's time by 0.40 hours.

Here's the general (unwritten) rule: Given a discrepancy in time billed, the senior biller's time will in *most* cases be assumed to be correct. So a partner's time would be assumed more accurate than an associate's time and an associate's time would be considered more accurate than the time billed by a paralegal.

And while deference is generally afforded to the partner, it's no guarantee that his/her time will not be challenged. In Example 2 above, the partner billed more time than the associate. Again, no one knows why, at least not from the time entry itself. But, given only a difference of 0.50 hours the partner time will more likely than not go unchallenged.

There are, however, situations when deference to the partner's stated time will be challenged as in the below example.

Example 4

> 05/05 Teleconference with client (C. Adams), partner (J. Thomas) and associate (K. Hughes) regarding strategy in light of denial of our Motion for Summary Judgment. [Associate D. Fowler]   0.70 hours

05/05 Conduct teleconference with client (C. Adams), associate (D. Fowler) and associate (K. Hughes) regarding strategy in light of denial of our Motion for Summary Judgment.   1.10 hours
[Partner J. Thomas]

05/05 Attend teleconference with client (C. Adams), partner (J. Thomas) and associate (D. Fowler) regarding strategy in light of denial of our Motion for Summary Judgment.
[Associate K. Hughes]   0.70 hours

In the above example, both associates billed the same amount of time whereas it was the partner who billed a different amount. The key isn't that partner Thomas billed *more* than associates Fowler and Hughes it's that he had billed a *different* amount of time. If Fowler and Hughes billed the 1.10 hours and Thomas billed 0.70 hours the conclusion would likely be the same, except that the Thomas' time would be cut in the former example and not in the latter example (since he billed less).

Discrepancies in amount of time billed at trial (as in example 3 above) are regularly observed by auditors. This is often due to block billing. One person includes their drive time back and forth from the courthouse, another person rolls in their preparation time and yet another person includes their communications after the day at trial ends.

The solution for most of these issues is a pretty simple one: At the end of any event in which multiple firm members attend the same event, take a moment and agree on the amount of time

ALL of you will bill. It's basically a foolproof method and if you are not doing it already you should do so immediately.

O. Premature and Unnecessary Work: Is it time to make the donuts?

Advance planning is admirable. Billing for work performed before it's necessary to do so is simply wrong. More often than not I see this play out in areas like trial preparation.

Example:

> Reviewed all correspondence and pleadings to date in preparation for trial.

On its face there's nothing wrong with that. However, if you've only had the case for three weeks it's fair to say that trial is anything but imminent — you have just filed your Answer and haven't even begun conducting discovery yet.

Then there are those who, almost immediately upon having same scheduled, will begin preparing for a deposition or hearing; even though it's two months away. If it IS necessary, then so be it — but you must make it quite clear why you're beginning so early if that's not clearly evident from the totality of the invoice.

While issues regarding premature tasks generally take place early in the case, questions regarding *necessity* tend to arise in the final stages of the litigation. Call it what you will — bad communication or bad case management, but nothing is worse than reviewing billing for unnecessary tasks performed *after* settlement has been reached...it's much more of a problem than you'd think. Summarizing depositions, extensive review of medical records, preparing jury instructions — the list goes on and on.

From a client perspective this looks bad. The firm appears disorganized. Again, this is not the way you want to close out billing on the matter. Don't tarnish a great result by being careless here.

Finally, auditors come across some entries where the narrative seems to be simply illogical.

Just a couple of my personal favorite examples:

Review status of all depositions taken.

Hmmm...if the depositions have already been taken, then what in the world does this mean?

Analyze missing discovery responses.

I'm not sure where to start here.

Suffice to say that your time entries are your responsibility. Treat them as seriously as the rest of the lawyering you are involved in and they will treat you very well. Give them short shrift and you will undoubtedly be short changed...that's the last thing I want for you.

Chapter 6

LAW FIRM STAFFING AND OFFICE COMMUNICATIONS

The Gang is All Here

Almost universally, client billing guidelines address early on what they consider to be a critically important subject: proper staffing of their cases. Given that overstaffing a matter can greatly increase their costs, it's no wonder that clients focus heavily on this.

Most clients start with the premise that one attorney should be primarily responsible for the matter. Generally, that person is a partner, but depending on knowledge/experience that person could well be an experienced associate attorney. Whoever he/she is, that person becomes the point person and primary contact for client communications. It's also typical that an associate attorney and a paralegal would be added to the team.

Of course, depending on the size of the matter, it's possible that literally dozens of people could be involved. Not surprisingly, with larger cases it's even more imperative that the matter be efficiently staffed. Doing so is a collaborative and sometimes difficult undertaking which requires tweaking and thoughtful consideration throughout the lifespan of the matter. The larger the staffing model employed, the greater the potential for duplication of efforts.

Duplication of Effort:

Q: How Many Lawyers Does It Take To Screw In a Light Bulb?

Answer: One. Unless it's a *really* big light bulb!

But seriously, it really does depend on how big a "light bulb" you're dealing with. The light bulb being analogous to the specific matter being handled. If your typical case requires one 15 watt bulb and another requires multiple 100 watt flood lights, you're going to need more help.

Just how much more help will depend upon many factors. If your client is involved in "bet the company" litigation you may have the equivalent of an entire football team (or two).

Let's say you're a second year associate. You ask yourself, "Why the heck should I care about all of this? I mean, the partner will be making the staffing decisions anyway, that's his problem, not mine."

The most successful staffing models have one thing in common — all of the professionals involved have identifiable and clearly defined roles. Furthermore, all of those individuals know precisely what their roles are and how each fits into the big picture of the case.

Your first responsibility is to understand what your role is and whether it's a static one or one that is anticipated to appreciably change during the pendency of the case.

While a good managing attorney will know precisely who is doing what and why, no one is infallible. Part of *your* job then, is to be aware to the extent possible what the rest of the team members are doing and to raise a flag whenever you spot duplication or inefficiencies of any kind. You don't want your four hours of research to get whacked if someone had previously researched the same issue.

But you don't have to spend four hours to run into a duplication of efforts problem. Far from it. If a notice of deposition arrives, you don't want multiple attorneys and paralegals billing to review it. Billing guidelines generally prohibit multiple attorneys/paralegals from reviewing the same document, particularly with regard to basic form documents and brief communications.

The issue is more complicated with larger documents including pleadings and various motions. Obviously, one person can invoice time for review and for my money (and yours) that should generally be the managing attorney. Beyond that, how many can bill to review the same document depends upon an observable need to do so.

Let's say that a Motion to Compel arrives and three attorneys bill to review it. That may look something like this example:

LAW FIRM STAFFING AND OFFICE COMMUNICATIONS

12/01 Receipt and review of plaintiff's motion to compel interrogatory answers.   0.40 hours
[Partner]

12/01 Review of plaintiff's motion to compel interrogatory answers.   0.50 hours
[Associate 1]

12/01 Analysis of plaintiff's motion to compel interrogatory answers.   0.40 hours
[Associate 2]

See a problem here? First, the auditor is not going to question the partner's time entry. The issue is the redundancy of both associates also reviewing the same motion. What's missing is an apparent need to do so.

But what if these entries were written as in the examples below?

12/01 Receipt and review of plaintiff's motion to compel interrogatory answers.   0.40 hours
[Partner]

12/01 Review of plaintiff's motion to compel interrogatory answers in preparation for researching cases cited in same.
[Associate 1]   0.50 hours

12/01 Analysis of plaintiff's motion to compel interrogatory answers in preparation for drafting reply motion.   0.40 hours
[Associate 2]

Both associates in the above example have a defined purpose for their review. You've made the auditor's job much easier and alleviated any concerns about duplication of effort. Having the purpose stated in the entry is far and away the best approach to avoid a duplication of effort issue.

But let's say the associates kept their original description as in the examples below.

> 12/01 Review of plaintiff's motion to compel interrogatory answers. 0.50 hours
> [Associate 1]
>
> 12/02 Began research of cases cited in plaintiff's motion to compel interrogatory answers. 1.90 hours
> [Associate 1]
>
> 12/01 Review of plaintiff's motion to compel interrogatory answers. 0.50 hours
> [Associate 2]
>
> 12/03 Began drafting reply motion to plaintiff's motion to compel interrogatory answers. 1.60 hours
> [Associate 2]

Here, while the associate attorneys failed to state the purpose of their review, the subsequent task performed clarifies that. As long as the auditor can follow the breadcrumbs, so to speak, by observing the performance of subsequent related tasks you should be fine. However, if it were my time (and my money) on the line I wouldn't leave it to careful auditing to discern the lack of duplication. **Always state the purpose and avoid the potential issue.**

LAW FIRM STAFFING AND OFFICE COMMUNICATIONS

Another problematic context for multiple billers occurs in the area of document review and is illustrated in the examples below:

Began review of plaintiff's document production.
[Associate 1]

Conducted review of plaintiff's document production.
[Associate 2]

Began careful review of newly received document production from plaintiff.
[Associate 3]

The issue should be immediately apparent. How can the auditor (or anyone for that matter) know who reviewed what portion of the document production? All three associates could have been reviewing the same documents, some of the same documents or completely different documents.

Being on the same page with your colleagues is critically important here and a little communication will go a long way to ensure that none of this time will be questioned. See the examples below.

Began review of plaintiff's document production (Bates range 1–203).
[Associate 1]

Conducted review of plaintiff's document production (Bates range 300–455).
[Associate 2]

Began careful review of newly received document production from plaintiff (Bates range 600–822).
[Associate 3]

With the above examples the auditor can readily see that all three associates were reviewing different documents. Instead of Bates numbers, batch numbers or simple page numbers could be used. As long as the auditor can differentiate who is reviewing what the chief concern about duplication of effort can be neutralized. I might add that this level of description, even in the absence of multiple attorneys performing the task, is something you want to incorporate in your personal billing practices.

Multiple Attendees: Two is too many — three is definitely a crowd.

Most billing agreements or guidelines specify that only one firm member can bill for attending the same hearing or deposition, etc., unless the client creates an exception and approves the additional attorney. While most of the time you're not going to be able to justify more than one attorney attending the same deposition or hearing, etc., there are times (excluding trial of course), where more than one attorney *is* justified. Perhaps the additional attorney is best suited to argue a different point in a Motion for Summary Judgment or appellate argument. The possibilities are endless. To be certain, your client is looking for your guidance to recommend actions which put them in the best position to be successful.

LAW FIRM STAFFING AND OFFICE COMMUNICATIONS

To that end, regardless of whether or not billing guidelines are in place, I encourage you to reach out to your client and explain the necessity of multiple firm members to bill for a particular event if the situation calls for it. If your reasoning makes any sense at all (and why wouldn't it?), you will likely receive approval without much question. Just don't abuse the privilege. By that I mean don't try to use this as an excuse for a new associate training opportunity. In fairness, I see evidence of this practice less and less nowadays.

From a nuts and bolts perspective, here are some things that you should be doing to ensure you get paid for multiple attendees:

(1) Make sure you note in your time entry that the client approved multiple firm personnel to attend the same event (Ex: "Multiple attorneys approved by adjuster R. Evans on 3/13"). There's no guesswork here.

(2) *Please* take the time to compare the amount of time that each timekeeper submits. All too often I see different amounts of time billed to attend a deposition or other event [See Chapter 5]. For instance, the partner bills 2.90 hours and the associate bills 3.20 hours. I'm going to lop 0.30 hours off the associate's time entry every time I see this. And how often do I see this issue? Unfortunately, almost every day.

(3) Description, description, description. If all you are doing is attending the deposition, you can certainly provide a description like, "Attend the deposition of A. Howard." However, if you are actively taking part, then make it clear that

you are doing so: "Attend and *participate* in the deposition of Plaintiff A. Howard." If you or the managing attorney obtained approval it must have been for good reason. Don't leave any doubt that the additional attorney was actively involved.

(4) Do not, I repeat, *do not* wait until after-the-fact to obtain approval for multiple attorneys to attend the same hearing, deposition, etc., for reasons I'll explain in more detail in the next chapter. But suffice to say that you're taking a risk that the time will not be paid at all.

Transient Timekeepers: Who Was That Masked Man?

When it comes to staffing, the bigger the case, the more numerous the pitfalls for the unwary. Efficient staffing is easier said than done and if not done carefully, overstaffing can result. These individuals may get lost in the shuffle at the outset of the case but a good auditor is going to detect an issue when they examine all of the timekeepers in isolation.

A transient timekeeper is one who (1) comes into the case only briefly and (2) does not appear to advance the matter in any appreciable manner.

These individuals aren't particular to any hierarchy within the firm; they could be partners, associates, of counsels or paralegals. A review of the tasks they perform finds them to be doing things like attending team meetings or reviewing the file, but not generating any identifiable work product. The inevitable question that arises is "Why is the person involved in this litigation?"

I can think of some reasons, however, why this could be the case. Perhaps there is a partner or associate with particular knowledge or experience and the one or two team meetings he/she attends are their opportunity to contribute to the matter in a unique way. And while that is a possibility, it's not the usual situation at all, at least not in this writer's experience.

How can you avoid this situation? Well, if you are the partner then you're the lucky person that has to keep a great scorecard and know and manage his roster well. If you have bit players on your team it behooves you to make it clear that their time billed reflected the need for their brief appearance (e.g., "[Partner] Attend and participate in team meeting to discuss strategic approach to questioning plaintiff's expert witness.")

Active participation is critical here. To the extent it can be clarified that what they bring to the case is unique, so much the better. The auditor will begin with the assumption that everyone involved is there for a good reason. However, if that person only bills once or twice in the billing period to "attend team meeting" you're not giving the auditor much of anything to work with.

If you happen to be the attorney or paralegal in question then you have a responsibility to ask the managing attorney or partner to clearly define your role. Although it shouldn't happen, if you find yourself in meetings or reviewing the file, but doing nothing more, alarm bells should be going off. There may be a very good reason why you're involved, but at the present stage in the litigation it's not apparent to someone looking at your firm's invoice. In that situation it's even more critical that your time entries clarify why you're involved (e.g., "Attend team meeting discussing background of case in order to draft Counterclaim."). There should never be any doubt as to why you are involved and what your part is in the matter.

Passive Timekeepers: Who Am I and What Am I Doing Here?

Unlike the transient timekeeper in the previous section, the passive timekeeper is an individual who consistently invoices fees to the matter. However, like the transient timekeeper, he/she does not appear to advance the matter in any meaningful non-duplicative manner.

These individuals primarily engage in reviewing the work product of others. In essence, their desk becomes a way station of sorts for paper to pass through but no more. They attend team meetings and conferences but rarely if ever generate any of their own work product.

Let's take a moment and look at "Fred." At first blush Fred appears to be actively involved in the matter. He certainly invoices a fair amount of fees and one would likely assume that he has a definable role to play in the case.

However, upon closer inspection that is not the case at all. He can be observed reviewing everything: Pleadings. Correspondence. You name it. It *all* lands on Fred's desk. I'm sure there's a very good reason why Fred is billing the client for his efforts. However, Fred has shown no evidence of any contribution to the case. He performs no affirmative actions. No drafting of any kind, no memoranda generated by his review, no office conference enlightening others who are *actively* involved in the matter with his assessment of the issue at hand or conclusions arrived at as a result of his review. Your client or their auditor is on the lookout for the Freds of this world. Don't be a Fred.

Like the transient timekeeper situation in the prior section, the responsibility for staffing falls squarely on the managing attorney. I'll be the first to concede that in more complex litigation he/she has quite a daunting task in efficiently staffing these matters and ensuring that each and every member of the team has a defined and non-duplicative role to carry out.

Regardless of whether the managing attorney is successful in that undertaking, if you are the passive timekeeper, or think you might be, then it falls on you to question your role or lack thereof. This is even more difficult than in the transient timekeeper situation because you will have more involvement. Therefore, it's easier to assume that you *must* have a defined role to play. After all, you've been tapped by the managing attorney to perform various tasks so why would you even think to question it? In the end, all you can do is make an honest assessment of what you are doing and how you fit into the picture. If multiple people are doing what you are doing, or if you are not generating any work product, then that's your sign.

Finally, while efficient staffing is the managing attorney's responsibility, it will be *your* own time that is cut, not his/hers. That should be incentive enough to take stock in your role and not be afraid to question it.

Position-Inappropriate Tasks:

Implicit in efficient and cost-effective staffing is the assignment of tasks to the appropriate personnel and level of expertise. Failure to do so in the context of hourly billing can result in overcharges to the client for tasks done by more senior firm members which could have been performed by lesser firm members; partners instead of associates, associates instead of paralegals and paralegals instead of administrative staff.

Examples:

Draft 1st Interrogatories and Production of Documents to Plaintiff.
[Partner]

Conduct factual research regarding weather conditions at time of accident.
[Associate]

Bates-stamp newly received document production from Plaintiff.
[Paralegal]

It should be clear in all of the above examples that the task was performed by firm personnel at the wrong level of expertise. An associate in most cases should be able to draft the initial discovery, while a paralegal would be more appropriate to carry out factual research, and Bates stamping is considered to be a clerical task not appropriate for any fee-generating staff.

Plenty of gray areas exist, but we are talking about work in which there would be general agreement that the individual performing the task was at a higher level than required to efficiently and competently perform same.

Again, it largely falls on the shoulders of the managing attorney to ensure that the work is performed at the proper level of expertise necessary to accomplish the specific task. However, there may be valid reasons why a partner may undertake a task that would typically go to an associate. If that is the case, it's in your best interest to explain your needed involvement (e.g., "Briefly conducted research in securities matter due to plaintiff's novel theory asserted in Complaint."). Would your client prefer to pay your partner rate for an hour of research it would take the associate five hours to do? Of course they would.

Finally, to the extent possible, it's *always* a great idea if you can put yourself in the shoes of the auditor. That's no less the case with regard to staffing issues like this. If you might raise an eyebrow and question why someone is involved in the task at hand, then absolutely assume someone else might do so as well.

Office Conferences: Talk is Not Cheap!

No one practices law in a vacuum. Some communication is absolutely essential. Attorneys and firm staff have to be on the same page in order to efficiently and effectively handle any case.

Despite this reality, your clients don't want you to bill time for this often-essential task. Or, more to the point, they strive to limit the situations in which they have to pay you for doing so, even though one very brief conversation picking the brain of a more senior attorney may prove to be valuable time spent (as well as money saved for the client!).

No matter — this is how it generally shakes out in real life regarding what clients will pay for — or not, as the case may be.

1) While this hardline approach is definitely in the minority, there are some clients that will *not* pay for office conferencing or memoranda at all. Personally, I think this is absurd. Unless you're flying solo, communication is an absolute necessity. You certainly cannot even manage a small team without it. So then, how the heck do you get paid with a flat-out prohibition against it?

As always, the old adage applies — the squeaky wheel gets the grease. I'm not talking about making a general complaint that the time you spend office conferencing should be compensable. In my opinion, the most forceful argument you can make is to cite the very guidelines that prohibit billing for this task. "Huh?" you say.

Without exception, even the most simplistic billing guidelines will stress that it is your responsibility to handle the case in the most efficient and cost-effective manner without compromising the quality and effectiveness of the representation.

Specifically, you should express your concern that at the very least you should be able to bill in instances where the expertise of a senior attorney is necessary in order to discuss matters of strategy. It's a reasonable request and most clients pay for this. You're arguing that billing a minimal amount of time for such activities is well worth it. This one conversation could prove to be pivotal in moving the case forward.

Remember, it's all about the client. You're trying to achieve the best outcome for them while being as efficient as you possibly can. Shouldn't a brief conversation that advances the matter on both fronts be compensable? Indeed it should.

You might be surprised to discover that they will carve an exception for you, regardless of what they prohibit in their billing guidelines. And if not, if enough of your brethren take my advice and make the same argument, it's a good chance that the next iteration of the billing guidelines will make a change to that effect.

Never underestimate the power you have to effectuate change with regard to this or, for that matter, any of the policies contained in the billing guidelines. Reasonable proposals for change are in most cases taken seriously. So don't sit back and grumble about it. Make your concern known. If you are successful in obtaining an exception for your time now, and especially if others join in voicing their concern, change *will* happen. I'm with you on this one.

2) The second variation, and most common in my experience, is the allowance of one attorney to bill his or her time for office conferencing "when the specific expertise or experience of another firm attorney serves to advance the matter." Additionally, the attorney providing that guidance should be the one to bill his/her time.

Here are a few examples of an acceptable (and therefore billable) office conference:

Example 1:

> Conference with associate T. Levin regarding suggested research strategy to bolster our argument on motion to dismiss.
> [Partner]

Example 2:

> Conference with associate G. Stallings regarding line of questioning for upcoming deposition of plaintiff's forensic expert R. Evans.
> [Partner]

These are clearly substantive in-firm conferences and should pass without any objections that I can imagine. I would be remiss, however, if I didn't include a word of warning about office conferences and the word "strategy." Some attorneys have the mistaken impression that including that word in their narrative means the time will automatically pass muster. Not so fast...

Example 3:

> Office conference with associate C. Squire regarding strategy.
> [Partner]

Please give the auditor something more to go on than that. "Strategy" with regard to *what*? That buzzword alone won't get you to the finish line.

LAW FIRM STAFFING AND OFFICE COMMUNICATIONS

Example 4:

Strategy meeting with associate T. Lee with regard to the proposed points of the argument for our Motion for Summary Judgment.
[Partner]

Well done. Just be aware that the word itself, while important, offers no immunity from having your time adjusted. However, a good narrative using the word "strategy" should link to the subject matter in a clear and unambiguous manner as in the above example.

Bear in mind though, the counterpart to the conference should be on the same page with the partner regarding the description of the discussion or you will potentially have an issue.

Example 5:

Strategy meeting with associate T. Lee with regard to the proposed points of the argument for our Motion for Summary Judgment.
[Partner]

In-firm conference with partner J. Cromwell with regard to motion.
[Associate]

The associate's entry lacks the specificity that the partner's entry does. I'm not saying that the partner and the associate necessarily need to precisely mimic each other's description. However, I am saying that the entries should reasonably resemble each other as to avoid doubts about the accuracy of one or the other. In practice, auditors will generally afford deference to the partner's description, but why leave any doubts? The message: Be descriptive and on the same page to the extent you can.

My best advice is to make it a habit not to leave any office conference without agreeing to both the amount of time and the subject matter of same. It would take you no more than a minute or two and that would be time well spent.

So, what is **not** a compensable office conference? Typically, it's what client billing guidelines refer to as office conferences that are "administrative, instructional or supervisory in nature." While it may not fit neatly into any of those categories, and well may be a blend of all three, partners assigning tasks to lower-level attorneys, associates and paraprofessionals are the most common of the prohibited office conferences that I routinely encounter.

Examples of non-billable office conferencing:

Office conference with associate regarding research assignment for motion to dismiss.

Provide instructions to litigation clerk regarding preparing trial binder.

Directive to associate to arrange and notice plaintiff's deposition.

The reality is that if you're only telling your associate to notice the plaintiff's deposition then I can't really tell you anything that will help you get paid for your effort. On the other hand, if the conversation were to involve anything to do with substantive law or some procedural strategy (hint, hint), then by all means, focus on *that*. Just make sure that your description contains enough detail to demonstrate that the meeting went beyond a simple instructional or supervisory communication.

Example:

> Conference with associate L. Wagner regarding arranging plaintiff's deposition and line of questioning in anticipation of same.

The secret here is that if part of the in-firm conference has an administrative component and the other part has a substantive one, the latter will in most cases negate the former and the conference will be a billable one.

3) There also are clients who will allow two attorneys and/or paraprofessional staff to bill for an office conference. God bless them. Generally, the more complex the litigation, the more this comes into play. The same fundamental criteria must be present. That is, the in-firm conference must include communications which demonstrate giving or obtaining advice on substantive or procedural aspects of the case.

Conferences between a partner and a paralegal or an associate and a paralegal more often than not fail to meet that threshold. This shouldn't come as much of a surprise to anyone given the nature of the tasks paralegals routinely perform. As a result, these discussions primarily involve the delegation of assignments.

This is unfortunate when you consider that some firms rely heavily on paralegal staff, which often draft basic pleadings, initial discovery requests, simple motions and conduct various research tasks, among others. Certainly some of that work would seem to potentially involve the need for more than mere instructional or educationally-focused discussion.

Examples:

[Associate] Conference with (paralegal) L. Anderson regarding case background and initial preparation of our interrogatory responses.

[Associate] Conference with (paralegal) V. Miller regarding unusual facts of the case and needed background research.

Contrast those descriptions with the following:

[Partner] Conference with (paralegal) L. Anderson regarding task to prepare interrogatory responses.

[Associate] Conference with (paralegal) V. Miller regarding assignment to conduct background research.

The latter examples appear to be no more than task-based discussions which could have easily been accomplished via e-mail. Whatever method used, such communications are clearly in the non-compensable bucket. This is in contrast to the former examples, which provide enough extra details to change the nature of the communication to a more substantive one. The goal is to show a "meeting of the minds" if you will, versus a meeting with the senior firm member telling a junior member what work to carry out.

It's a finer line than one may think initially. Again, if the in-firm conference is no more than a "do this, do that" discussion, then it is what it is. If it's anything else, take a few extra moments to thoughtfully describe the meeting and ask yourself if it would meet the client's threshold or not.

4) Finally, some client billing guidelines do not specify any limitations on the number of in-firm attendees. The same foundational requirements apply here as well: All of the conferees must be essential to the discussion and their role in the litigation must be clearly defined.

The team meeting is a common feature of complex litigation but it comes with its own set of potential issues. The problem arises when the firm bills individuals who only have a minor or undefined role in the litigation. While the team meeting often serves a valuable purpose, too often I see individuals whose sole contribution appears no more than to bring the doughnuts. A quick review of their other billed time reveals that they are bit players of sorts, and that their role is ill-defined at best and often duplicative of the efforts of others.

The team meeting invariably includes a paralegal who typically describes his/her time as "take notes from meeting and distribute to partners and associates." However critical those notes are, this is one instance where you can expect to have the time cut. This is a good opportunity for the billing partner to exercise some billing judgment and weed this time out rather than forcing the auditor to do so.

Why? Well, it's evidence that you are actively engaged in managing the cost aspect of the case. It tells your client that you are cognizant of their bottom line — you can never go wrong here. Again though, include the time on your bill and show that you've written it off. The additional benefit is that it shows the auditor (and client) that what remains on the invoice has been evaluated by you and therefore *should* be payable. It says that the other conference attendees are essential and that any review of their overall entries will bear that out.

The Uncharged Office Conference

Aside from the problems caused by different timekeepers billing differing amounts of time to the same in-firm conference, nothing is more problematic than the confusion that can be created by the uncharged office conference.

The following example illustrates the problem.

Example

> 09/23 Conference with partner R. O'Reilly regarding potential Motion to Dismiss.   0.40 hours
> [T. Carlson]
>
> 09/23 In-firm conference with associate V. Dunn regarding upcoming deposition of plaintiff's forensic expert and strategy for same.   0.70 hours
> [R. O'Reilly]
>
> 09/23 Office conference with partner R. O'Reilly regarding strategy with regard to questioning in next week's deposi-

LAW FIRM STAFFING AND OFFICE COMMUNICATIONS

tion of plaintiff's forensic expert. 0.70 hours
[V. Dunn]

In the above example, partner O'Reilly billed for his in-firm conference with associate Dunn but not for the conference with associate Carlson. Was this an oversight? Did he write the time off for some reason? Who knows? I mean, why wouldn't he bill for it if he could? But, for our purposes let's assume he can.

Auditors look at in-firm conferences and try to match up the participants. The above entry by associate T. Carlson becomes problematic because he was the only party billing to it. Either the associate didn't really have a conference with the partner or the partner didn't bill for it for some unexplained reason.

Let's add another nuance to the problem as is illustrated in the below example.

Example

09/23 Conference with partner R. O'Reilly regarding potential Motion to Dismiss. 0.40 hours
[T. Carlson]

09/23 Draft e-mail to associate T. Carlson regarding basis for Motion to Dismiss. 0.20 hours
[R. O'Reilly]

09/23 Review e-mail from associate T. Carlson regarding potential Motion to Dismiss. 0.20 hours
[R. O'Reilly]

This example shows the uncertainty caused when communications don't line up. If there are two conferees, each is a bookend of sorts. When one bookend is missing, flashing lights start to go off for the auditor as a myriad of possibilities are in play.

Did the associate substitute the word "conference" for an exchange of e-mails? If so, why? If the partner drafted an e-mail to the associate and reviewed an e-mail from the associate then why didn't the associate's time on that day reflect same?

The point of all this is that by creating doubt, confusion or uncertainty with respect to these communications, you are doing a disservice to yourself and the firm. Building trust with the client is your prime directive.

It's my goal for you to avoid creating any uncertainty about the accuracy of your billing because I've witnessed firsthand the damage that can result. Take note of the above and you will be light years ahead of some of your colleagues, but most of all, you will put yourself in the best light by being perceived as an honest and careful biller. It will be worth your effort — guaranteed.

Chapter 7

BILLING JUDGMENT, BILLING GUIDELINES AND APPEALS

Understand, Plan, Prevail and Prosper

Billing Judgment: Do You Have It?

I grappled with whether or not to open the book with this subchapter but ultimately concluded that it would be more effective to include it at the end, after we've examined some of the most common legal billing pitfalls in which attorneys wittingly or unwittingly find themselves.

We start with the premise that attorneys have a fiduciary duty and that duty is breached when an attorney bills for unnecessary services or overcharges fees. *See Coughlin v. SeRine*, 507 N.E. 2d 505, 515 (111. App. Ct. 1987). Furthermore, "[t]he falsification in any manner of bills to clients is unethical and reprehensible. Billing practices, like every other aspect of client dealing, should be conducted in a scrupulously honest manner." *Florida Bar v. Herzog*, 521 So. 2d 1118 (Fla. 1988).

We proceed on the basis and assumption that the majority of legal professionals wouldn't dream of billing for unnecessary services or intentionally overcharging their fees and that they do their best to bill in a "scrupulously honest manner." That would be *you*.

So what, then, is billing judgment and why do we care about it?

As the court in *In re Leonard Jed Co.*, 103 B.R. 706, 713, 714 (Bankr. D. Md. 1989), stated:

> "Normally, counsel who represents a private client exercises what the courts refer to as 'billing judgment' by 'writing off' charges for certain things." The records of the firm did not "evidence the exercise of any billing judgment in that nothing appears to have been written off. In the absence of such evidence, the court will exercise its own billing judgment by writing off various efforts which ought not to have been charged to the estate as being either totally non-productive or of negligible benefit."

In my experience I can unquestionably state that the degree of billing judgment exercised by counsel appears to have substantially increased over the past 5-10 years. I believe this trend is not only in response to more and more clients having billing guidelines and a formal audit process in place, but also due to firms taking a more proactive approach when dealing with billing issues.

From its humble beginnings roughly 30 years ago, the legal bill review industry has grown considerably. You'd be hard-pressed to find a client of any size that doesn't have some form of audit process in place (but if you do find one, please send them my way.) It's only a guess because I haven't been standing in your shoes for a long time now, but I can only surmise that firms are tired of having someone writing off their time. I'm not sure who said it, but sometimes you have to get to the point where you are "sick and tired of being sick and tired." A goodly number of firms have reached that point.

I've also seen a greater effort by firms to educate their attorneys, paralegals and administrative and support staff with regard to proper billing. I'm asked more frequently by firms to speak with their staff and attorneys regarding best practices and meeting or exceeding their client's expectations. And those efforts are literally paying off. The number of pristine invoices coming in for me to review appears to be steadily increasing.

Yet for some firms and certain individuals at otherwise excellent billing firms, the work to get in line with client billing expectations is far from over. Moreover, their efforts with regard to billing judgment are inconsistent or in some cases are completely lacking, as is evidenced by the entries below which I've recently evaluated. All make you wonder whether or not the bills received any serious review by the firm before being sent to the client.

BILLING JUDGMENT, BILLING GUIDELINES AND APPEALS

Examples:

Overbilled time   1.30 hours

I have no idea what this referred to. But I am sure that at least 1.30 hours was overbilled to the client.

Inaudible   0.90 hours

My best guess here is that the attorney's legal secretary couldn't understand his/her dictation of the time entry but billed it anyway rather than asking the attorney for clarification. This also means the partner did not read the bill before it was sent to the client. Unfortunately, a common mistake.

Purchased book   1.80 hours

I'm still wondering what that book is. Needless to say, such an entry should never be billed to a fee paying client. Well, unless you purchased *this* book. (Sorry, I couldn't resist!)

Bible   0.70 hours

No, the firm in this verb-less example did not bill the previous entry — that could have helped solve the mystery, though. Of course, the moral is that legal billing and mysteries do not go together well at all.

No narrative in Firmware   1.20 hours

Well, hey, who needs a narrative anyway if you know how much time the attorney billed?

Spoke with Lisa regarding depo preparation materials
                                                  0.50 hours

There's only one problem with this time entry. The attorney who billed for the discussion, is named Lisa and apparently billed to speak with herself. Talking to yourself may be considered by some to be a sign of high intelligence, but when it comes to legal billing, take my advice and avoid billing your client for doing so.

To be fair, the above examples are decidedly atypical. But I point them out in order to highlight that by exercising a modicum of billing judgment, many problematic entries should be easy to identify and modify as necessary.

Aside from obvious nonsensical and vague entries, the task gets increasingly difficult from there. That type of thing can (and should) be fixed, but when it comes to administrative and clerical work, cutting the time can be more challenging. While it should be relatively easy to make the call to cut entries for things like opening a file or printing documents, I can certainly understand the inclination to bill for them anyway. For one, there's really no way to rehabilitate the work to make it compensable anyway, so either the firm cuts it or the auditor does. Why not make them do the hard work? Perhaps the auditor will be asleep at the wheel and the time may squeak through?

Let's remember the core directive of billing judgment: *You should be writing off work which should not be passed along to the client.*

Either through your knowledge as applied to the client's billing guidelines or plain common sense, it's incumbent upon you to identify problematic entries before the invoice ever goes out.

I also wholeheartedly recommend that instead of removing the entries you include them with a big "N/C" in parenthesis at the end of the narrative. Of course, don't do this for any time that you would be embarrassed to share (like the above nonsensical entry examples). However, I don't consider it a mistake to include any other time which would be non-billable as long as you actually do not bill for that time. It's verifiable proof that someone at the firm is exercising billing judgment. But please don't forget to actually cut the hourly fee at the end of the entry. It happens rather frequently that I see an "N/C" but at the end of the narrative the firm nonetheless charged the client for it anyway, giving me an easy adjustment and making the firm appear disorganized. If you include the "N/C" make sure that is precisely what you have done.

Billing Guidelines: Know the Rules & Win the Game

Depending on your time in practice, chances are you already have read and been required to adhere to a boatload of client billing guidelines. If that's the case, then you already know that to a large extent, if you've seen one, you've seen them all. That's not to say that there aren't differences, as there most definitely are. It's been my job to apply dozens of client billing guideline requirements over the years as well as draft and revise new guidelines for many of those clients. What you'll find (if you haven't already) is that by and large, the core tenets of most have nearly the same provisions in place. The wording may be a bit different, but you'll see very similar descriptions of what is expected and what is prohibited.

This is good news, because when moving from one client's work during your day to another, you've already got the basics internalized whether you realize it or not. Let's review some of those basics (we've covered a number of the major topics previously).

1. Hourly Legal Fees

A) Block Billing

You know what it is by now. The prohibition is nearly universal and quite simply the biggest avoidable billing error you could make. Do one task, bill for one task. Rinse and repeat. [SEE Chapter 1 for further details and examples].

B) Administrative Tasks

Administrative tasks are those which generally involve the day-to-day functions in the administration and management of a law firm (overhead) and therefore do not constitute legal work which may be invoiced to a fee-paying party. This is a standard billing guideline prohibition disallowing work billed for such things as conflict checks, invoice preparation, scheduling activities, general management and training. [SEE Chapter 4 for further details and examples.]

C) Clerical Tasks

Clerical tasks refer to activities which do not generally require legal acumen or experience. Like administrative work, these are considered to be firm *overhead* tasks which should not be passed along to the client. As such, you will find a universal guideline prohibition against billing work such as printing, faxing, scanning and organizing documents, creating binders and other secretarial tasks. [SEE Chapter 4 for further details and examples].

D) Vague Task Descriptions

One of the chief requirements included in any set of client billing guidelines is the duty to provide complete and accurate information. Not including same makes any effort at understanding the nature of the work performed and evaluating its merit to be difficult if not altogether impossible. It should be self-evident that uninformative descriptions such as "work on matter" and "telephone call" are inadequate. [SEE Chapter 2 for further details and examples].

E) In-Firm Conferences

Another standard provision found in nearly all client billing guidelines is some sort of language regarding who, if anyone, can invoice time for in-firm meetings and conferences. That language runs the gamut from an outright ban on billing for such conferences, to allowing an entire team to do so under certain circumstances. Billable conferences and meetings have one key component: that they involve a substantive discussion of the law and/or procedural aspects of the case at hand. In the absence of same, such communications will typically be deemed non-compensable. [SEE Chapter 6 for further details and examples].

F) Multiple Attendees

A central concern of most clients is duplication of effort on the part of the firm. The most obvious situation is two or more attorneys billing to attend the same hearing, deposition, meeting or other event without any apparent need or justification for doing so. In order to avoid that situation, most clients include guideline language requiring pre-approval for multiple firm members to attend the same event. [SEE Chapter 6 for further details and examples].

G) Staffing

With regard to the subject of staffing, most client billing guidelines provide that the matter should be staffed by one primary attorney along with another attorney (if needed) at a lesser rate and/or a paralegal. The overriding goal is efficiency and the avoidance of duplication of efforts. Larger matters will unavoidably require more personnel. It's critical for the firm to convey to the client the necessity for additional staffing and to define the roles for each of the proposed team members. [SEE Chapter 6 for further details and examples].

H) Orientation

Another standard provision common to most billing guidelines is a prohibition against billing time for replacement lawyers or paralegals to get up to speed in the matter. The thinking being that the client should not be penalized when people working on the case leave the firm or are no longer available. I've always considered this to be a weak rule and potentially quite unfair. God forbid the managing attorney has a heart attack or is stricken with a serious disease. Whose fault is that? What if the shoe were on the other foot? If the claims or other client representative quits or gets sick are you going to refuse to get *them* up to speed? Of course not! Fortunately, I find this rule to be one which is rarely utilized. Also, there is also usually an exception included for situations in which the client has requested a specific person to assist in the matter. Finally, though, if you have any concerns when such a situation arises, reach out and explain the circumstances. Especially in illness scenarios, they would be jerks to deny a reasonable amount of time for someone to become acquainted with the matter. If there is an emergency situation where someone has to quickly get acclimated in order to handle a deposition or hearing, then note that on your bill. I'm with you on this one.

I) Proper Billing Increments

It would be rare indeed to find a set of client billing guidelines which did not require that time be calculated to the nearest tenth (0.10) of an hour. Gone are the days of quarter-hour (0.25) billing, although on occasion I still find a few attorneys doing so. Nothing unusual or unexpected on this point. I would imagine that the vast majority of you have been billing in tenths of an hour since you began your legal careers. Just keep on doing what you have been doing.

J) Rate Increases

Another standard billing guidelines rule is that the client will not accept any bills containing *unilateral* rate increases. As I've stated before, bill audit software offers little assistance to the auditor other than keeping track of basic numbers and data (e.g., that you've billed 27 hours in the same day or that you double-billed an entry or an entire invoice). The other thing it does and does well is flagging time billed at unapproved hourly rates. If you bill electronically (and you probably do) the program will catch any rate discrepancy every time.

I'm surprised at the number of invoices I come across that have this issue. Unless those higher rates have been approved by the client, the invoice will be adjusted to the existing approved rates. Expect no leeway on this. No one gets a pay raise without going through a process of some kind and it's no different here. Your client expects to have a meeting of the minds when it comes to compensation.

While I can't tell you how to approach that meeting other than to tout your wins and other accomplishments, I can tell you that there is often an amazingly large disparity with regard to rates for doing essentially the same work. Sure, some of that can absolutely be attributed to regional differences, but I'm talking about apples to apples comparisons here; firms in the same area with the same area of expertise and roughly the same size. All I can say is that if you think you've earned the increase or if it's been quite a while, then go for it! I see some firms go five years or more without a rate increase and I say to myself "What are you guys waiting for?" One thing is absolutely certain; if you don't ask for the increase, the client won't be coming to you offering one.

BILLING JUDGMENT, BILLING GUIDELINES AND APPEALS

K) Tasks Requiring Approval

You can count on requirements in most billing guidelines that certain tasks and/or actions must be pre-approved in advance. Multiple attorneys attending the same event, billing over a certain amount of hours in one day, performing legal research and/or doing so over a certain number of hours, conducting a deposition, drafting a counterclaim, third-party claim or dispositive motion, hiring an expert or obtaining an independent medical examination — these are some of the rules you may encounter depending on the client, their lines of business, and the type of litigation that they require representation for.

While there may be a lot of rules, the positive aspect from my experience, is that most reasonable requests involving variances to these rules are well-received and more often than not, accepted. You're providing the guidance and you have your client's trust. Their natural inclination then, is to be receptive to any well-reasoned recommendation you present which will further their interests. So, by all means, make your case. Also, don't fail to get pre-approval for tasks outlined as requiring pre-approval. Any perceived hassle will be worth it and you'll avoid the audit unpleasantries for not doing so. There's nothing worse than conducting ten hours of research and having seven of those hours cut for not obtaining pre-approval for research time over three hours.

L) Tasks Billed at Proper Level of Expertise

As a corollary to staffing issues, clients are, not surprisingly, concerned about work not being performed at the proper level of expertise. Specifically, partners performing associate level work, associates performing paralegal level work and paralegals performing secretarial work.

1) Partners/Associates

This is easier said than done in light of the high potential for overlap. Especially in the partner-associate realm there are no easy bright-lines to follow. Taking the position that a partner, for instance, can *never* do x or y task is both unreasonable and short-sighted. Sure, some generalizations can fairly be made, but absolutes here are neither desirable nor practical. For instance, drafting a Motion to Compel should be a task suitable for most associates, but are we saying a partner couldn't invoice any time reviewing or revising the motion? Absolutely not.

Guidelines generally couch these directives in language citing cost-effectiveness and efficiency without compromising quality. And I can fully understand the impulse to regurgitate the "you get what you pay for" cliché here. Speaking of which, the rules in this area typically specify that if a partner performs an associate level task then he/she should bill for that task at the lower associate rate. If you're wondering at all about compliance on this point, in practice I can honestly relate that self-policing in this regard is virtually non-existent. That is, I have not witnessed partners *voluntarily* reducing their rates to a lower associate rate or associates reducing their hourly rate to a paralegal rate. It just does not happen. However, the auditors I've known tread very delicately here and for good reason. These are not easy calls to make. That said, we do make them from time to time so these directives should not be ignored, either.

2) Paralegals

While billing guidelines are rather general about attorney tasks and what would be more appropriate for an associate versus a partner, they are usually very specific about what they consider to be paralegal-level work.

Examples of such work includes: Preparing form discovery requests, drafting subpoenas and simple notices, cite-checking case law, drafting page-line deposition summaries, conducting factual research, preparing hearing or trial binders, medical chronologies and drafting medical or other authorizations, to name only a few. Guidelines typically state that if an attorney performs these tasks he/she should reduce their rate to the firm's paralegal rate. Additionally, most guidelines provide that review and revision, especially of pleadings and discovery documents **are** billable at the attorney rate.

It's my observation that most firms do a good overall job in ensuring that such tasks are performed by paralegal staff. However, adjusting their rates downward when attorneys do perform such work is as rare or nonexistent as partners reducing their rates to associate rates when they perform associate-level work. But while auditors will shy away from classifying work performed by a partner as associate-level work, there is far less hesitancy to do so when attorneys are performing tasks client billing guidelines label as paralegal tasks. It's in this situation that the majority of adjustments are made and therefore it's the situation you should be most concerned about.

Despite the commonalities, there is no substitute for knowing the particulars of the billing guidelines for whatever client you are performing work for. You may be assigning the cite-checking task to a paralegal without needing to do so. Despite the similarities in guidelines from one client to another, the *differences* are what can derail your efforts. So whether you're the managing attorney assigning the work, or an attorney or paralegal undertaking the work, the responsibility is no less yours to be aware of the requirements before you assign or undertake any task.

M) Long Billing Days

While covered in more detail in Chapter 5, the main point here is that the vast majority of client billing guidelines will have a set limit on the number of hours which can be invoiced in a single day. While typically eight (8) hours, some guidelines will permit as many as ten (10) hours in a day without approval from the client. Guidelines being exactly that, exceptions are naturally built in for trial, travel, pleading deadlines and other circumstances requiring time beyond the stated maximum number of hours. Please also be aware that even *with* approval, many clients will still have an upper limit on the number of hours which can be billed in one day. I've seen anywhere from twelve (12) to sixteen (16) hours. You should know what these limits are in order to avoid a significant potential reduction.

BILLING JUDGMENT, BILLING GUIDELINES AND APPEALS

N) Travel

Also covered in more detail in Chapter 5, there are quite a few variances from one client to the next regarding what they are willing to allow with regard to fees billed when you travel, and it pays to know what those differences are.

1) Air/Rail Travel
   - No fee billing permitted.
   - Fifty (50%) percent of fees allowed.
   - One-hundred (100%) percent of fees allowed.
   - Only reimbursable if work is performed during flight.

2) Automobile
   - No fee billing permitted.
   - No fee billing for local travel (e.g. under 50 miles).
   - One-hundred (100%) percent of fees allowed.

The best practice here (assuming you can bill fees) is to state the purpose of the travel and the destination.

> Flight from NYC (LaGuardia) to Chicago (O'Hare) for continued deposition of plaintiff expert L. Samuels and prepared for same during flight by reviewing first deposition and outline.

> Travel by automobile from Alexandria, LA to 5th Circuit Court in New Orleans, LA for appellate argument.

In summary, be as specific as possible and avoid uninformative narratives such as "Travel to Philadelphia."

2. Legal Billing: General Requirements and Issues to Avoid

A) Frequency of Billing

The vast majority of clients require monthly billing and most firms do a fine job in meeting that expectation. And why wouldn't they? Everyone I know wants to be paid on time. Despite that, there are some firms who, for whatever reason, struggle with this or are inconsistent. This runs the entire gamut from large law firms to mom and pop outfits. I understand that things sometimes fall through the cracks, but collecting money you are owed shouldn't be one of them, especially since your client wants to get you paid.

Yet, it's not uncommon in my world to see an invoice that is one or two years old. Because of budgetary and accrual considerations, those tardy billing firms are making things harder for the client. When it comes to expenditures, companies like as much certainty as possible, just like the rest of us. Also, they may have already closed the claim or matter and now they will have to re-open it and possibly have to obtain more reserves to make the payment(s). Because of this, more and more clients are imposing stiff penalties for late billing. It's not unheard of to have clients completely disallow or severely reduce a bill that is a year old or more. And even if they do not, trust me when I tell you that they will be greatly annoyed. And aside from the potential financial loss for the firm, there is the unwanted perception that you don't have your act together. It's a big unforced error that you can do without.

BILLING JUDGMENT, BILLING GUIDELINES AND APPEALS

B) Itemization of Expenses and Backup Documentation

No doubt most of you have to provide detailed expense reports replete with receipts when you are seeking reimbursement from your own firm. Your client has the same expectations and billing guidelines universally bear out that fact. Itemization of all expense charges is standard procedure as is providing the corresponding backup documentation required to substantiate those charges. It's my observation that most firms do a fine job with the itemization part but sometimes fall short when it comes to providing the documentation.

While failing to do so is not the end of the world, it nevertheless creates needless extra work for the firm because you'll have to appeal and/or re-bill the expense. And if you don't do so in a timely fashion, you may end up eating those expenses. I suspect that the cause in some cases is that the billing clerk is chasing various people for receipts. Whatever the reason, this should be a rare or non-existent occurrence for the firm if you have good procedures in place.

C) Online Legal Research

The days of billing your client for Westlaw or Lexis charges for online legal research is pretty much over, and rightly so. The old law library has become a dinosaur and online research is now considered by clients to be part of the firm's overhead costs. I occasionally see some firms try to slip these charges in but they are wasting their time. This is simply one of the costs of doing business.

D) Non-Billable Expenses

Charges for standard postage, telephone and cell phone charges and faxes are for the most part items that your clients won't pay for. Additionally, billing for things like office supplies and conference room charges are also generally not billable. On the other hand, most clients will pay for express mail (FedEx, UPS) when those services are necessary. The key is to be judicious about when to utilize those services.

E) Travel/Transportation Charges

If there is a general theme here, it's *reasonableness*.

- Hotels

With regard to hotel charges you don't have to stay at a cheap dump in the bad part of town, but you shouldn't be booking rooms at the Ritz either. Many client billing guidelines will specify a maximum nightly rate, so be aware of that, if you're not already. In practice I see very few firms billing for staying at budget motels and a fair number of firms pushing the boundaries with regard to luxury hotels. Admittedly, the challenge can be tougher when you need a room in NYC or Washington, DC, for instance. Obviously, book in advance to the extent practical and if there are no rooms in the location where you need to be, and the rates are higher than what the client specifies, then by all means explain that to them. You're taking care of *their* business and they have a vested interest here. No one wants you in a potentially unsafe location; they only want to make sure you're not living the high life on their dime. While you're at it, please do not include any mini-bar charges on your invoice or charges for

BILLING JUDGMENT, BILLING GUIDELINES AND APPEALS

alcohol whatsoever! If there's one pet peeve that sets off clients, it's when the firm bills them for alcohol. Even if they are part of the celebration with you after a win, don't include it on your bill. I've seen business relationships ruined or damaged over this, so don't let this easily avoidable situation happen to you.

- Airfare

The rules here are quite straightforward. Most guidelines allow economy and some even allow business class flights but none will allow billing for first class airfare. If you have a modest up-charge for extra leg room, no one is likely to bat an eye at that. Baggage fees and other incidentals are usually allowable, although in-flight internet charges may not be. If you're working during the flight, I would recommend putting a note by the internet fee stating "Worked on matter during flight [see narrative]."

- Ground Transportation

Charges for taxis and services like Uber and Lyft are billable, but skip the limousine or "black car" services if you want to be paid. For appropriate circumstances, car rental charges are generally allowable unless you rent a Porsche or a Lamborghini. If you're driving your own car, then mileage at the present IRS rate is fair game.

F) Expert Retention

I have never witnessed this guideline requirement to be an issue but suffice to say that you should never retain an expert without discussion with and approval from your client.

G) Staff Overtime or Temp Fees

Administrative staffing is a law firm responsibility. If your legal secretary has to work overtime or if you hired a temp because of the volume of work on your client's case, that's part of the firm's administrative overhead; it's not your client's responsibility. Most billing guidelines provide as much. If there is good news here, it's that if your administrative staff is working longer hours, then your fee-generating staff likely is as well.

H) Other Expense Charges

A corollary to the above overtime (pay) prohibition is billing for additional charges related to the functioning of the law firm's premises. Passing along costs for things like extra HVAC and electric to the client is not permitted in most cases. Again, these are the costs of running a business. Besides, if you have to crank on the A/C on a Sunday because you're ramping up for trial, those extra hourly fees should more than make up for any additional energy usage.

I) Billing Summary

Standard language in any set of billing guidelines is the basic requirement that your invoices contain the full name of the timekeeper, his/her position/rank, their hourly rate and the total number of hours billed. If issues arise in this area they usually involve smaller firms which are generating paper invoices versus doing electronic billing. These paper invoices sometimes leave out one or more of the required elements. For instance, "Lisa Smith" might be billed as "L. Smith." In other cases she may simply be billed as "attorney" instead of "associate attorney" or "partner/shareholder." Fortunately, it's rare that a firm will not include the billing rate or number of hours worked, but it does happen on occasion. The point is that these are simple and understandable billing guidelines requirements to meet. It would be a shame to have your invoice rejected for not including this information.

J) UTBMS Billing Codes

If there's one thing I can commiserate with you on, it's the requirement that your time entries must include the appropriate task and activity codes. I'm referring to the American Bar Association Uniform Task-Based Management System (UTBMS) Litigation and Activity codes (L & A codes) for fees or the expense code (E codes) for expenses.

Let's say you draft an Answer and instead of using code L210 (Pleadings) you use code L240 (Dispositive Motions). From an audit perspective will your time be reduced or disallowed? Will your invoice be rejected if in fact *every* code you choose is the wrong one? My answer is an emphatic "No!"

I've yet to read and/or apply a client's billing guidelines which prescribed any penalty for using the codes incorrectly. Not that I'm encouraging you to disregard this requirement, but I can only imagine the countless hours attorneys spend laboring over which code to use. But what I can say is that you certainly shouldn't obsess over which code to utilize. Frankly, it's not worth your time. The clients I've worked for, if they've used the information at all they have generally used it for data mining purposes to ask such questions as "How much of last year's legal spend went for written discovery and how much went for trial costs?" In my nearly 20 years as an auditor I haven't spent one minute checking to see if even one attorney used the right code or not. Take it for what it's worth.

Alternative Billing Arrangements

Although beyond the scope of this book, it's worth noting two methods which could potentially help you avoid most of the rules and requirements which you have to keep track of and adhere to in order to comply with any client billing guidelines.

A) Flat Fees

Depending on the nature of the work you perform and the specific client, this may be an attractive option if you've done your homework and the client is receptive to alternative billing ideas.

Both you and your client want certainty. They want to be able to plan for litigation costs as best as possible and you want to know that your invoice will be paid in full and not dissected eight ways from Sunday. In fairness, these goals may be much easier to achieve if you're doing personal lines defense for an insurance carrier as opposed to IP work for a technology company. However, if you're dialed into your firm's data you should have a very good idea of where you need to be from a profit perspective.

You can assume that many of your clients have quantified the range of costs for things such as Answer preparation, drafting and responding to discovery, drafting various motions, conducting depositions and trial costs. For the most part they have a good idea as to a range in costs for each of these specific legal tasks/phases and what the differences are between firms.

It behooves you to know what those numbers are as well, for two reasons. First, without doing the analysis, you'll never know if such an arrangement even makes sense for your firm or not. Going through the process may inform you of wide disparities between firm members who perform the same or similar tasks. You may even learn that you're not billing enough in some cases. As the saying goes, "Knowledge is power." It's your business; having your finger on the pulse of it is the best way to keep it healthy and thriving.

The second reason is that the client may be the one who approaches you with the flat fee idea. If that is the case, you can assume that they have done all of the background slicing and dicing concerning precisely what you bill for any given task, as well as any specific phase of litigation. If they're coming to you with a flat fee proposal you can further assume they that have determined that it's in *their* best interest if you accept. However, the only way you'll know if that proposal makes sense for your firm is if you've put forth the time and effort to do the assessment on your own beforehand. Not that you can't trust their data, but having your own gives you a basis to point out any flaws in theirs. Besides, it's *your* work. No one should know it better than you do.

Finally, flat fees don't have to be an all-or-nothing proposition either. They can be limited in scope so it may well make sense to reach an agreement with regard to fees for one or more specific tasks versus an entire case. Again, you'll never know unless you conduct an assessment. If it were my firm it would be standard practice.

B) Complete Exemption

You may or may not be surprised to learn that some firms have managed to negotiate a complete exemption from the requirements of their client's billing guidelines.

Make no mistake; this is a highly unusual situation. However, I have witnessed firms pull it off. To do so there are three essential criteria that needs to be present:

1) Your firm needs to be perceived as a "go to" firm for the client. That is, if they could only work with one firm or a handful of firms your firm would be on or at the top of that list.

2) Your firm needs to have impeccable billing. I'm talking about no billing issues whatsoever and an adjustment rate at virtually 0% which validates the lack of billing issues.

3) Relationships, relationships, relationships…The managing attorney needs to have an unusually close relationship with the decision-maker on the client side.

Without all three factors in alignment, your chance of success is nil. You could be the "go to" firm because of your overall results but still not have stellar billing. On the other hand, you could have average case results and be a model firm when it comes to billing. But even if you meet both of those criteria you'll not likely gain any traction with a proposal of this nature if you don't have a superlative relationship with the client's decision-maker.

So why would the client agree to such an arrangement?

First, it costs money to pay auditors to review billing. Additionally, the client typically pays licensing fees for the software used by the auditors. Those charges are based on the gross amount of fees and expenses which are submitted through the billing portal. If your firm is billing significant amounts of money and the auditing efforts aren't yielding tangible results, then the client is not receiving any value for their money. In effect, it's costing them to audit you. How much does it cost them? I've seen anything from one-quarter percent (0.25%) to three percent (3%) of the total fees reviewed.

Your first job is to know what *your* numbers are, that is, your adjustment numbers. Every firm has a hiccup here and there despite their best efforts. But if your firm is under one-tenth of one percent (0.1%) you are golden. That would mean less than $1000 adjusted for every million dollars billed, or $100 or less for every $100,000.

If you meet that standard you've rounded first base and are on your way to a standup double. What I can't help you with is the case results prong, but you should be keenly aware of how you stand up on that aspect. *If* the results are excellent you're now on third base and whether you come "home" or not boils down to relationships.

Let me tell you a little secret. Yes, your client does not want to overpay in legal fees, they want to be treated fairly, but if it was up to them they'd throw the billing guidelines and the auditors they hire overboard in a heartbeat if they believed they could. Why? Because it strains relationships. By and large their internal staff (claims representatives and in-house attorneys) hate it, as do (not surprisingly) the law firms who work for them.

So if you have the results, the low adjustments and an exceptional relationship with a decision-maker, you have nothing to lose by making a proposal. My suggestion would be to propose something to the effect that they would spot check your invoices over a period of six months to a year. By doing that, you're saying that nothing will change, that your outstanding billing will continue, but that you want to reassure your client nothing will change by proposing verification of that fact at any point. By seemingly having nothing to hide, (and you don't!) this disarming approach may be your ticket.

Yes, it's a long shot. However, if your firm has the right stuff, then you have a marvelous opportunity. If you're successful, you can use this as leverage to approach your other clients. Can you imagine being able to tell them, "Yeah, did you know that XYZ Corporation thought our billing was so stellar that they exempted us from their billing guidelines audit process?" I'd be impressed.

Successfully Handling Appeals of Audit Adjustments

While it is my goal for you that you never have to appeal an auditor's adjustment, especially after implementing and applying the information and advice preceding this section, it's unrealistic to assume it never will happen. Despite your best efforts

BILLING JUDGMENT, BILLING GUIDELINES AND APPEALS

and use of billing judgment, time entries will occasionally slip through that you wish you could get back. But it's not only you. To be sure, auditors make plenty of mistakes. However, the vast majority of those I know are, above all, intellectually honest. We respect you. Most of us are lawyers as well and we can easily put ourselves in your shoes.

That said, not every client has an auditor. You can have claims representatives, paralegals and various management staff engaged in the process. In those circumstances, consistency and reasonableness can take a back seat. You quickly realize that you're better off with an attorney/auditor who has a better understanding of what you do and how you do it versus someone who doesn't and then willy-nilly slashes your bill for some nonsensical reason. Worse yet, rather than a formal report detailing any billing infractions, you may get your bill back with chicken-scratch hand-written in the margins.

But we're getting a little bit ahead of ourselves here. For those new to this entire process you may be asking yourself what exactly an appeal is.

Billing guidelines provide your client's substantive rules and procedural framework for getting law firm invoices paid. Failure to follow those rules and procedures can result in adjustments to various fee and expense entries. Given that those adjustments are made without consultation with the firm, and acknowledging that adjustments can be made in error or through misunderstanding, guidelines uniformly include an appeal process for the firm to challenge those adjustments.

But before we get to the nuts and bolts of handling appeals, it is incumbent that you make sure your firm has its own process in place to achieve optimal results. While these may be basic suggestions, they will ensure that it's far less likely that the ball is dropped and that you fail to respond to the appeal in an appropriate and timely manner.

1) Your firm has up-to date contact information to receive the initial audit report.

It's not uncommon for me to receive a call or an e-mail from a firm asking why the payment for their invoice was less than the full amount. My first question is usually "Did you receive our Invoice Non-Compliance Report?" The response in a fair number of instances is that they did not. And the culprit in many of those cases is that the firm's designated contact is no longer at the firm. In rarer instances, the client either had inaccurate contact information to begin with or none at all.

If there's any good news with regard to the above, it's that if the firm didn't receive the report to begin with, then the clock to respond will be reset out of fairness. Obviously, you can't respond to something you haven't seen. In cases where there has been a significant passage of time, the client will sometimes agree to refund the invoice adjustments as a matter of good will, especially if they failed to verify a valid contact to begin with. If you honestly didn't receive the report and the client isn't willing to recognize that, then you have quite an issue. If you are not afforded an opportunity to respond then you are due a full refund. Period.

BILLING JUDGMENT, BILLING GUIDELINES AND APPEALS

When it comes to your contact information, redundancy is good. Most audit software programs allow reports to be automatically sent to multiple contacts. Remember that time is of the essence. The clock is running. If your contact is out sick or on vacation you can't afford to miss a beat. I'd recommend designating both the primary billing clerk for that client as well as the primary attorney for the client.

2) Know the appeal response time period for each of your clients.

Typically, client billing guidelines provide that the firm will have thirty (30) days to respond or appeal any adjustments made by the client and/or their auditors. The clock starts running the day the audit report is emailed to the designated contact(s) at the firm. There are variations on the time period to respond; I've seen as little as 15 days and as many as 60 days. Additionally, guidelines will often allow a second appeal although some will not.

If you're not doing this already I recommend keeping a very simple chart like the one below handy in order to keep track of the appeal response time period for each of your clients.

Client/Company	Number of Days to Appeal Bill Adjustments	Number of Days for 2nd appeal of Bill Adjustments
ABC Holdings	30	30
Earth Corporation	15	15
Morris Insurance	60	30
ZXY International	30	n/a

While some clients may give you a little bit of leeway on the timing, never count on that. This is your statute of limitations, if you will. Therefore, it's critical that you're on top of this. All too frequently I have to break the news to the firm that their appeal is out of time and cannot be considered. I don't want that to happen to you. You deserve the opportunity to appeal, but you won't get that opportunity if you're not timely with your response.

3) Have a system in place for each of your clients.

What I'm talking about here is a flowchart of some kind which displays the internal route the audit report will take to completion of your response to each client. While that, of course, starts with your designated contact or contacts, where will the report go from there and how will that be accomplished?

If you're a small firm and the same three attorneys and paralegals work each matter, the task is far easier than a 100 member firm in which 15 people may bill at various times to one matter. The challenge arises because not only are more timekeepers involved, but depending upon the invoice period, adjustments may be made to different timekeepers each time. And (this is important), it should be obvious that the timekeeper who received the adjustment should be the one to address that adjustment. He/she did the work and wrote the time entry; therefore they are in the best position to respond to the client and/or their auditors.

How your firm chooses to route and keep track of all this can surely be a daunting task. I can only imagine that someone,

BILLING JUDGMENT, BILLING GUIDELINES AND APPEALS

in all likelihood the billing clerk, is quarterbacking the process and has the unenviable job of keeping a multitude of balls in the air at the same time. Suppose that five timekeepers received adjustments on a particular invoice. And that's just one invoice for one client. Multiply this out to multiple invoices for a number of clients and the billing clerk's task becomes analogous to an air traffic controller. Sure, no one is going to die if one of the "planes" gets lost in the shuffle, but one missing response or blown appeal deadline could cost your firm thousands.

Your basic flowchart may appear to be something like this:

a) Audit report received by firm contact(s), usually that client's billing coordinator.

b) Audit report reviewed by contact(s) for substance of adjustments and timekeepers involved.

c) Email sent to respective timekeepers with report and time period to provide responses to same.

d) Responses collected from timekeepers and collated to prepare the firm's appeal response.

My recommendation is that the managing attorney for the client in question to be included in the process even if he/she did not receive any adjustments. Why? Because the managing attorney needs to be aware of the issues involved and whether or not something needs to be taken up directly with the client. They also need to be aware of which of their timekeepers are having difficulty with the billing guidelines and whether or not the billing issues are ones that keep resurfacing or are new problems altogether.

4) Respond with a Unified Voice

I recall a situation in which the attorney's time was adjusted down to a paralegal rate for performing the paralegal task of drafting a basic subpoena. Her client's guidelines provided that drafting a subpoena was a paralegal-rate task. Therefore, when the attorney billed to draft the subpoena her time was reduced to the firm's paralegal rate. Her response was "only an attorney can issue a subpoena in the state of _____."

That's all well and good, I thought, but why is it that the other eight partners and associates who bill this client have no problems with the same adjustment — but she did? She suggested it would be malpractice on her part to allow it, because the paralegal would be unlawfully engaged in the practice of law. However, no other firm member shared her concerns or appealed the very same adjustments. This did not mean that her concerns and argument were not valid. However, since the rest of timekeepers who were adjusted acquiesced, her position was not effective.

What, then, to do? If, for example, five of you work for the same client, take a few minutes each month and meet to discuss the billing results. You'll quickly identify the issues the auditor is flagging. Decide what you want to contest, but more importantly, decide what the firm position is on each issue and stick with that. Be consistent and apply the rationale to each and every invoice the firm handles for that client. While having a unified voice may not guarantee the desired result, it will force the auditor to reexamine the issue and possibly even create an exception. At the very least it will put you in the best position to win on the issue you are challenging.

5) The "Nuts and Bolts" of a Successful Appeal Response

a) The Best Appeal is the One You Don't Have to Write

Let's suppose your recent bill to ZXY Company is reduced by their auditor for $5,000 due to billing activities identified as clerical tasks. The work was related to downloading voluminous documents from the company and uploading them to a document review platform, along with various other technical non-legal tasks. While these tasks are addressed in the company's billing guidelines as non-billable work, you recall that you discussed this with the client and came to the agreement that the work would be compensable, not only for this matter but for several other similar large matters that would be upcoming.

Even if no such discussion took place or agreement was reached, I have a novel suggestion for you. Pick up the phone and call the auditor and have a conversation about it. It is amazing that the vast majority of attorneys will not do this. The benefit to you is three-fold. (1) You may not have to go through the tedious process involved. (2) You may be able to reach an understanding as to how similar work in the future will be treated, and (3) You'll have the opportunity to build a working relationship with the auditor.

I can't stress the importance of the last benefit. If (like me) you ascribe to the old adage "the squeaky wheel gets the grease" then you understand what I'm saying here. If you're not keen on appealing every issue in writing this method has tremendous value potential for you. While you may still have to submit a formal appeal for reimbursement purposes, it's far easier to write "Work billable per discussion with _____ on _____" than having to argue the issue in writing and possibly getting nowhere with it for your efforts. I've personally witnessed a 5-minute phone call resolve endless back and forth appeals that otherwise went nowhere. It's hand-down one of the best "calls" you could make.

b) Do Not Entrust Appeal Responses to the Billing Coordinator

I have a confession. Some of the nicest people I've met in the legal world work in firm billing. The majority of these people are hard-working conscientious individuals doing their best to accomplish any number of critical tasks to ensure that your firm is paid. They're working with numerous billing systems that all have their own nuances and they have to be as well versed in each of the client billing guidelines as you are. But, as capable as they are, they should not be drafting responses to appeals.

Most importantly, they didn't do the work. So they can't possibly know what the attorney or paralegal did in order to address the issue. I can usually immediately spot instances where this happened. They are forced to respond with generalities that often completely miss the mark or fail to provide a satisfactory rationale for overturning the adjustment. In other instances it's clear to me that they've been provided with some information from the attorney or paralegal, but not enough information to clarify the work performed or point out a fallacy with the auditor's logic.

I don't mean to suggest that your billing clerk or coordinator cannot respond to any aspect of an appeal. Issues regarding things like timekeeper rates and expense documentation are entirely suitable and should be performed by these individuals. However, when it comes to the appeal of fee entries, the response should only come from the timekeeper who performed the work, as they are unquestionably in the best position to fully address those issues.

c) Avoid Using Boilerplate or Terse Language to Respond to an Appeal

I'd be curious as to what your experience is on this point, but when I receive an appeal response like the example below it rarely goes well for the firm:

> This is not clerical work and we expect payment.

First off, the auditor determined that the task was a clerical one and cited the client's billing guidelines in explaining why. However, nothing in the firm's appeal response addresses why that conclusion was incorrect. It may indeed be incorrect, but simply making a bald assertion that such is the case won't fly. And adding that "we expect payment" is not only ineffective but counterproductive to reaching your goal. Instead, be as specific as possible:

> We disagree with the basis of the adjustment. While our paralegal did gather the hearing transcripts, her primary task was to review and highlight relevant sections of each transcript in order to reduce the attorney's time billed to prepare for the upcoming arbitration.

On appeal, the firm clarified that the original time entry ("Gathered hearing transcripts in preparation for upcoming arbitration.") was *accurate, but did not include the substance of the task*, which was to review and highlight the transcripts to reduce the attorney's preparation time. Remember that all the auditor has to go by is the description your firm provides. The additional details were essential to changing the character of the task performed from a non-billable one to a billable one. However, *changing* the substance of the task performed altogether is quite problematic, as discussed in the section below.

d) Do NOT change the substance of the task performed on appeal

I'm hoping my experiences are in the minority and perhaps an aberration, but increasingly I've observed some firms re-tooling their time entries on appeal in order to meet the client's expectations regarding what is billable work.

Below is an example of the original entry which was adjusted.

Printed and organized MSJ for attorney review.

Even in the absence of billing guidelines, printing documents is not a billable task. And as far as organizing an MSJ, I'm unsure as to what that would mean with respect to a fully drafted motion. On appeal the firm simply rewrote the time entry and provided no comment or explanation as shown below.

Drafted exhibits for MSJ.

BILLING JUDGMENT, BILLING GUIDELINES AND APPEALS

In situations such as this I always ask the following question, "Does the time entry on appeal bear any reasonable resemblance to the original time entry submitted to the client?"

In this example, my answer would be an emphatic "No!" I hope you would concur.

In general, auditors proceed on the assumption that the original time entry most accurately reflects the work performed, discounting, of course, entries using ambiguous or vague language which did not convey the true and accurate nature of the work performed, or which were otherwise clear except that pertinent information was omitted, as with the prior example.

In our example, the auditor would rightly in my view assume the task involved exactly what was submitted on the invoice, that the timekeeper "printed and organized [the] MSJ." If the paralegal had drafted exhibits for the MSJ why wouldn't she have stated that? Note that the firm isn't saying that the paralegal drafted the exhibits *in addition to* the printing and organizing, but is instead asserting that the new description was the *sole* task performed.

This puts the client and their auditor in a difficult situation. No one wants to call anyone a liar, and to be sure, they're not going to say that; either the paralegal drafted the exhibits or she printed and organized the motion, or she did both. As I recall, my response to the firm was essentially my initial question to you phrased as a conclusion — that is, "The response on appeal does not bear any reasonable resemblance to the original time entry submitted to the client." In case you're wondering, the firm did not respond. While this is not conclusive, virtually 99.99% of the time in similar scenarios in which this is my response the firm will not submit a 2nd appeal.

The takeaway for you is to take your losses if and when they are appropriate. Additional information is fine, wholesale changes generally are not. Use billing judgment and write off time for non-compensable work and move on to the work you have a chance to be successful in addressing.

Finally, some firms will appeal virtually every adjustment to their invoices. And while that is certainly their prerogative, their arguments can come across as diluted when they challenge everything. Invariably, weaker responses are included which often end up detracting from their stronger (winning) arguments. While I can't fault them for trying, I find firms that are more selective tend to have a better success ratio.

e) Look for Inconsistencies in the Auditor's Rationale

Your initial thought here might be that I'm going to suggest that you point out inconsistencies in which the auditor flags the very same task on one invoice, but not on another. And while that point may be 100% correct, it won't do much in most cases to advance the ball for *you*.

While auditors strive to be consistent, they are going to miss things; it's the nature of the beast. There may be other reasons as well. Some clients set minimum dollar thresholds at which invoices will be audited. Other clients may employ a random methodology. The fact is that the client won't inform you of any of these things. You may also be unwittingly inviting unwanted scrutiny in the process. So while I completely understand the impulse to make this argument, it's not in your best interest to do so.

The inconsistencies that I suggest you focus on concern the **rationale** or characterization of the non-compliant task which was the subject of the adjustment. It's important to note that many clients will employ multiple auditors. In those situations you will invariably find more inconsistencies in rationales for the same adjustments as opposed to when only one auditor is involved. Either way, it's a *certainty* that you will find them.

Let's look at a simple example to illustrate the point.

Invoice #101

Drafted Pro Hac Vice Motion and all supporting documents.

This entry was adjusted for "position-inappropriate" task. A partner drafted the motion and the auditor adjusted her down to the associate rate, stating that the task should have been performed by an associate or billed at the lesser associate rate.

Invoice #202

Drafted Pro Hac Vice Motion and all supporting documents.

The above subsequent firm invoice (in another matter) contained the identical entry which was adjusted to zero by the auditor, stating that the task was administrative in nature and therefore non-billable. The unstated rationale being that the firm/attorney could not have handled the matter without being able to practice in the jurisdiction to begin with. That is, it is a cost of doing business; firm overhead if you will.

The "Inconsistency" Argument

> We find the auditor's basis for the adjustment to be inconsistent. Previously, our drafting of a PHV motion was characterized as a position-inappropriate task which required our partner to delegate the task to an associate or bill at the lesser associate rate. On the present invoice the auditor asserted that the task was administrative and therefore entirely non-billable.

To make this argument, you would have to be aware of the inconsistency between invoices. My recommendation is that you have your staff keep a database of adjustments by category (e.g., administrative, block billing, clerical, etc.) for each of your clients. Granted, you probably won't have the luxury of time to review everything, but looking at a few prior examples could be well worth it. Better yet, this task could be researched by your staff with audit discrepancies highlighted for future appeals. I consider this to be a hidden gold mine of sorts. It's an approach I rarely see, but I can assure you (shhhhh!) the inconsistencies are there to be found. Finding them and pointing them out is a super-effective strategy.

The "It's Not in the Guidelines" Argument

> We note that the specific task adjusted was not addressed in your billing guidelines. Drafting the Pro Hac Vice Motion was not an administrative activity. On the contrary, it was a purely legal task requiring an attorney and was necessary

> to represent your insured in this matter. As such, we respectfully request compensation for this work.

Guidelines are exactly that and cannot address every possible scenario. The adjustment which is the subject of our discussion here is one of those. Adjustments for issues not explicitly stated in the guidelines offer better opportunities for successful challenges. However, this approach requires more than pointing to the task as not being one which was explicitly addressed in your client's billing guidelines. Barring obvious inconsistencies or flat out errors, you will find that your client's auditor(s) in most cases will be open to reasoned arguments for issues not directly addressed in the client's guidelines. Fundamental fairness requires that your client does not hide the ball when it comes to their expectations and I can happily report that most pride themselves on doing just that. In the absence of a clear-cut rule, you have an open opportunity to present your side of the argument on what may be an issue of first impression.

The "We had Pre-Approval" Argument

> When discussing the new matter with claims adjuster A. Smith, we discussed the PHV motion and Smith asked us to proceed.

Newsflash #1: In general there is a very little communication between the client's claims representative or their in-house attorney and the client's auditor regarding special agreements with the firm. So, the situation here should be an easy layup and slam dunk for you. The fact is, the auditor is often the last one to know and I can tell you that it's a great source of frustration for those of us in this industry.

Newsflash #2: It is not uncommon to come across cases in which the claims rep or in-house attorney agrees to an exception that the auditor would *never* agree with. In my experience, when this happens they will rarely backtrack from their agreement with the firm. Good news for you, bad news for the auditor.

The "This Doesn't Make Sense" Argument

To be sure, you are of course going to be far more tactful than that. Just like auditors come across nonsensical time entries, you will on occasion come across nonsensical auditor adjustments and corresponding explanations accompanying them. The auditor may have intended to address another entry, copied the wrong canned language from his comment cheat-sheet, or had a brain freeze. Mistakes happen.

You're going to receive a written report listing all non-compliant billing entries and the reasons why the auditor has come to the conclusions he/she has. Let's say that the auditor characterized the Pro Hac Vice Motion as a "Non-Billable Office Conference." You don't have to rub their nose in it; state the fact and the response will speak for itself.

> We disagree with the characterization of our drafting of the Pro Hac Vice Motion as a Non-Billable Office Conference and request the charges for same be paid.

BILLING JUDGMENT, BILLING GUIDELINES AND APPEALS

In response to your appeal, most auditors will readily acknowledge these errors and will not deny your appeal on the basis of "I really meant to say x or y." If the auditor completely missed the mark, they will generally not use this as an opportunity for a second bite at the apple. Most of the time the acknowledgement will be self-evident — you'll be paid for the previously disallowed time and the only response (if any) you will receive back is for entries which the auditor has denied on appeal.

In still other cases, the auditor may admit the error but also use this as an opportunity to put the firm on notice regarding their stance with regard to the task at issue. In that case, you'll also be paid for the time but you'll have to fight the issue another day. The smart move here is not to wait, but to be pro-active. Do an end-run around the auditor and go to your client contact and make your case regarding the task before the same task appears on another bill. If your position regarding the work appears reasonable you'll generally find that you get a positive response. Remember that in the tripartite relationship which includes you as the outside counsel, the client's representative, and the client's auditor, it's the auditor that is often the odd man out. Use that to your advantage, my friend.

In summary, you have many tools and approaches at your disposal like the ones above. I can't stress upon you how much power you have. While every client is looking to save money, their first instinct is not to accomplish that by making the firm's wallet lighter. It may appear that way, but it is most certainly not so in most cases. Above all, they have rules to follow and similarly expect that you follow theirs. Should there be unfairness in the latter, by and large they are open to rectifying that. Yes, they may be writing the check, but they are relying on *you* to help them avoid writing a much bigger check to someone else.

About the Author

David Schrader is a former practicing attorney who has spent nearly 20 years as a legal auditor, working directly for Fortune 500 companies and insurance carriers and also as a third-party legal auditor covering diverse areas of law. He is passionate about his work and speaking with legal professionals about how they can improve their billing. *Getting Paid. Legal Auditing and Your Bottom Line* encompasses much of that experience as well as his desire to share with and educate those in the profession about best practices in this area.

David lives with his wife Elizabeth outside of St. Louis and enjoys mountain biking, playing the bass guitar, their Great Pyrenees and traveling to their two favorite places – Wyoming and the Gulf Coast of Florida.

If you have any questions about the book or about legal auditing, David can be reached at davids@legalauditingexpert.com.

Made in the USA
Lexington, KY
13 November 2019